Text-Based Writing

Grade 2

Manufacturer Evan-Moor Corporation
10 Harris Court, Suite C-3 Monterey, CA 93940, USA
www.evan-moor.com

EU Rep. Authorised Rep Compliance Ltd., Ground Floor,
71 Lower Baggot Street, Dublin, D02 P593, Ireland
www.arccompliance.com

Editorial Development: Renee Biermann
Cindie Farley
Lisa Vitarisi Mathews
Copy Editing: Cathy Harber
Art Direction: Cheryl Puckett
Art Management: Kathy Kopp
Cover Design: Yuki Meyer
Illustration: Ruth Flanigan
Design/Production: Susan Lovell
Jessica Onken

Evan-Moor Educational Publishers

EMC 2452

Visit
teaching-standards.com
to view a correlation
of this book.

Correlated to Current Standards

Congratulations on your purchase of some of the finest teaching materials in the world.

For information about other Evan-Moor products, call 1-800-777-4362, fax 1-800-777-4332, or visit our website, www.evan-moor.com.

10 Harris Court, Suite C-3, Monterey, CA 93940-5773. Printed in USA.

002

CPSIA: Globus Printing & Packaging, Minster, OH, USA [2/2026]

Contents

What's in Every Unit?

For the Teacher

Resource pages outline lesson objectives and provide instructional guidance.

The reading level helps identify appropriate texts.

Lesson objectives and content-area concepts are indicated.

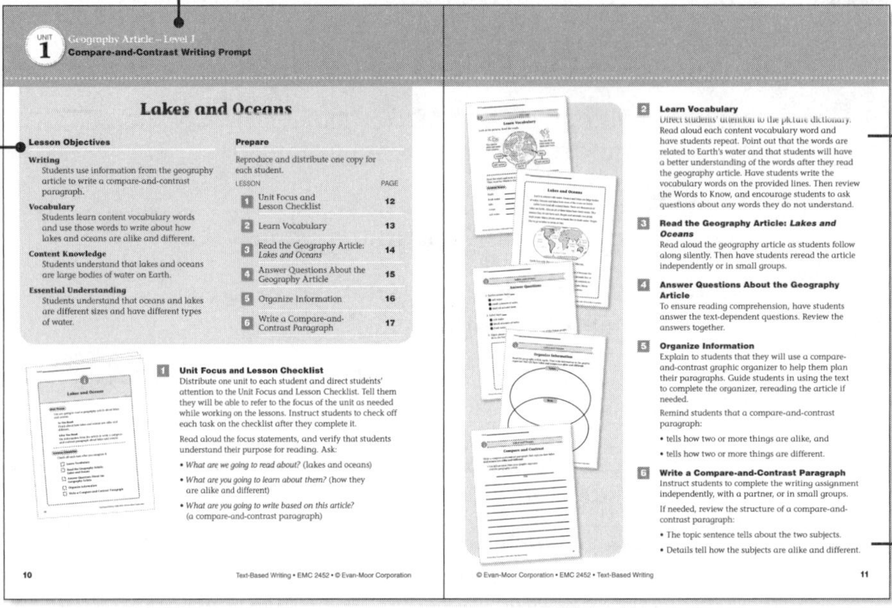

UNIT 1 Geography Article – Level J
Compare-and-Contrast Writing Prompt

Lakes and Oceans

Lesson Objectives

Writing
Students use information from the geography article to write a compare-and-contrast paragraph.

Vocabulary
Students learn content vocabulary words and use those words to write about how lakes and oceans are alike and different.

Content Knowledge
Students understand that lakes and oceans are large bodies of water on Earth.

Essential Understanding
Students understand that oceans and lakes are different sizes and have different types of water.

Prepare
Reproduce and distribute one copy for each student.

LESSON		PAGE
1	Unit Focus and Lesson Checklist	12
2	Learn Vocabulary	13
3	Read the Geography Article: *Lakes and Oceans*	14
4	Answer Questions About the Geography Article	15
5	Organize Information	16
6	Write a Compare-and-Contrast Paragraph	17

1 Unit Focus and Lesson Checklist
Distribute one unit to each student and direct students' attention to the Unit Focus and Lesson Checklist. Tell them they will be able to refer to the focus of the unit as needed while working on the lessons. Instruct students to check off each task on the checklist after they complete it.

Read aloud the focus statements, and verify that students understand their purpose for reading. Ask:

- *What are we going to read about?* (lakes and oceans)
- *What are you going to learn about them?* (how they are alike and different)
- *What are you going to write based on this article?* (a compare-and-contrast paragraph)

10 Text-Based Writing • EMC 2452 • © Evan-Moor Corporation

2 Learn Vocabulary
Direct students' attention to the picture dictionary. Read aloud each content vocabulary word and have students repeat. Point out that the words are related to Earth's water and that students will have a better understanding of the words after they read the geography article. Have students write the vocabulary words on the provided lines. Then review the Words to Know, and encourage students to ask questions about any words they do not understand.

3 Read the Geography Article: *Lakes and Oceans*
Read aloud the geography article as students follow along silently. Then have students reread the article independently or in small groups.

4 Answer Questions About the Geography Article
To ensure reading comprehension, have students answer the text-dependent questions. Review the answers together.

5 Organize Information
Explain to students that they will use a compare-and-contrast graphic organizer to help them plan their paragraphs. Guide students in using the text to complete the organizer, rereading the article if needed.

Remind students that a compare-and-contrast paragraph:

- tells how two or more things are alike, and
- tells how two or more things are different.

6 Write a Compare-and-Contrast Paragraph
Instruct students to complete the writing assignment independently, with a partner, or in small groups.

If needed, review the structure of a compare-and-contrast paragraph:

- The topic sentence tells about the two subjects.
- Details tell how the subjects are alike and different.

© Evan-Moor Corporation • EMC 2452 • Text-Based Writing 11

A suggested learning path helps you pace the lesson.

For the Student

Student pages provide unit focus, organizational tools, nonfiction content, and skills practice.

1 Unit Focus and Lesson Checklist

The Unit Focus provides a purpose for reading.

The Lesson Checklist guides students through the learning path.

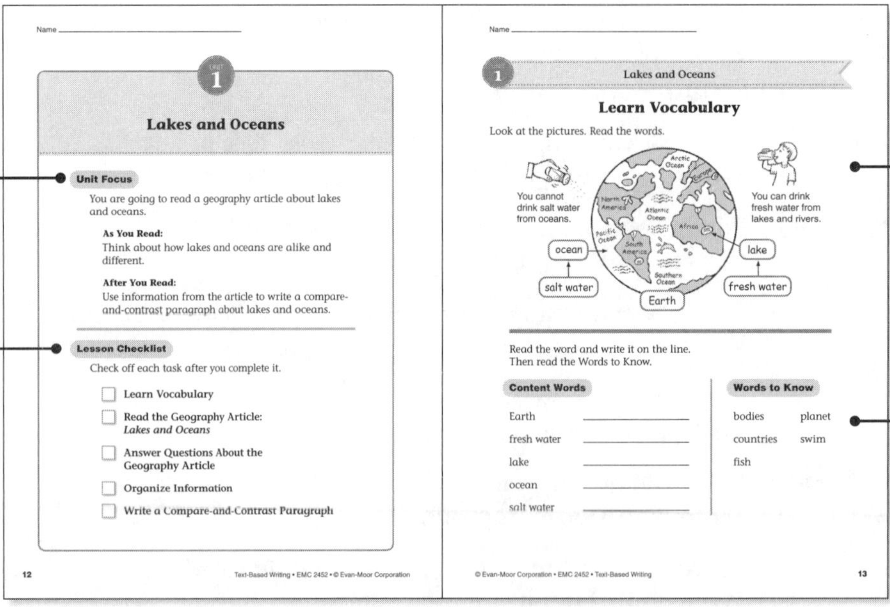

Name ____________

UNIT 1

Lakes and Oceans

Unit Focus
You are going to read a geography article about lakes and oceans.

As You Read:
Think about how lakes and oceans are alike and different.

After You Read:
Use information from the article to write a compare-and-contrast paragraph about lakes and oceans.

Lesson Checklist
Check off each task after you complete it.

- ☐ Learn Vocabulary
- ☐ Read the Geography Article: *Lakes and Oceans*
- ☐ Answer Questions About the Geography Article
- ☐ Organize Information
- ☐ Write a Compare-and-Contrast Paragraph

12 Text-Based Writing • EMC 2452 • © Evan-Moor Corporation

Name ____________

UNIT 1 Lakes and Oceans

Learn Vocabulary

Look at the pictures. Read the words.

Read the word and write it on the line.
Then read the Words to Know.

Content Words		Words to Know	
Earth	________	bodies	planet
fresh water	________	countries	swim
lake	________	fish	
ocean	________		
salt water	________		

© Evan-Moor Corporation • EMC 2452 • Text-Based Writing 13

2 Vocabulary

A picture dictionary provides visual cues and helps students connect words with meanings.

Additional vocabulary words are identified.

3 Nonfiction Article

A short text introduces a content-area topic and provides details.

Illustrations and graphics provide additional information and context.

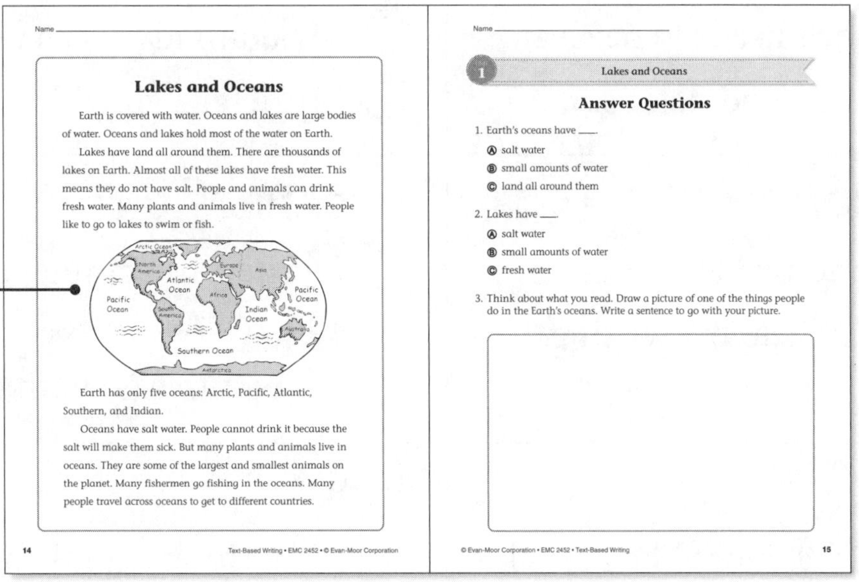

Name

Lakes and Oceans

Earth is covered with water. Oceans and lakes are large bodies of water. Oceans and lakes hold most of the water on Earth.

Lakes have land all around them. There are thousands of lakes on Earth. Almost all of these lakes have fresh water. This means they do not have salt. People and animals can drink fresh water. Many plants and animals live in fresh water. People like to go to lakes to swim or fish.

Earth has only five oceans: Arctic, Pacific, Atlantic, Southern, and Indian.

Oceans have salt water. People cannot drink it because the salt will make them sick. But many plants and animals live in oceans. They are some of the largest and smallest animals on the planet. Many fishermen go fishing in the oceans. Many people travel across oceans to get to different countries.

14 Text-Based Writing • EMC 2452 • © Evan-Moor Corporation

Name

1 Lakes and Oceans

Answer Questions

1. Earth's oceans have ___.
   Ⓐ salt water
   Ⓑ small amounts of water
   Ⓒ land all around them
2. Lakes have ___.
   Ⓐ salt water
   Ⓑ small amounts of water
   Ⓒ fresh water
3. Think about what you read. Draw a picture of one of the things people do in the Earth's oceans. Write a sentence to go with your picture.

© Evan-Moor Corporation • EMC 2452 • Text-Based Writing 15

4 Comprehension Questions

Text-based questions appear in multiple-choice and constructed-response formats.

5 Graphic Organizer

A graphic organizer helps students organize information from the article to plan their writing.

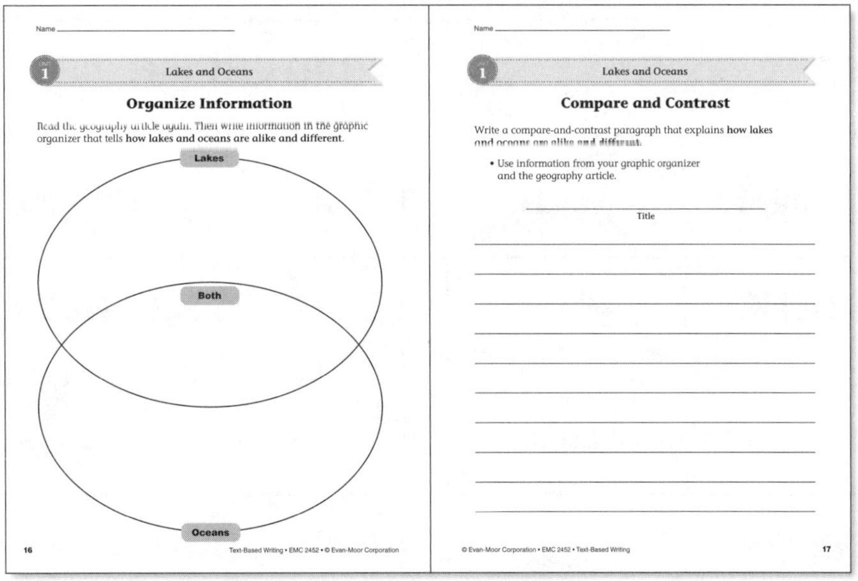

Name

1 Lakes and Oceans

Organize Information

Read the geography article again. Then write information in the graphic organizer that tells **how lakes and oceans are alike and different.**

Lakes

Both

Oceans

16 Text-Based Writing • EMC 2452 • © Evan-Moor Corporation

Name

1 Lakes and Oceans

Compare and Contrast

Write a compare-and-contrast paragraph that explains **how lakes and oceans are alike and different.**

- Use information from your graphic organizer and the geography article.

Title

© Evan-Moor Corporation • EMC 2452 • Text-Based Writing 17

6 Writing Prompt

A text-based writing prompt helps students synthesize what they've learned.

Student Rubric

I Can Improve This	I've Got This!
IDEAS ☐ My main idea needs to be clear. ☐ I need to add good details.	**IDEAS** ☐ My main idea is clear. ☐ My details go with the main idea.
ORGANIZATION ☐ I need to put my ideas in order. ☐ Pictures will help my writing.	**ORGANIZATION** ☐ I write a beginning, a middle, and an end. ☐ My pictures go with my writing.
VOICE ☐ I need to write more like I speak. ☐ My writing can do its job better.	**VOICE** ☐ My writing sounds like me. ☐ My writing does its job.
WORD CHOICE ☐ I need to use stronger words. ☐ I need to change hurtful words.	**WORD CHOICE** ☐ I use interesting words. ☐ My words are polite.
SENTENCE FLUENCY ☐ I need to fix my sentences. ☐ I need to use more time words.	**SENTENCE FLUENCY** ☐ I write complete sentences. ☐ I use time words.
CONVENTIONS ☐ I need to fix my spelling. ☐ I need to fix my grammar. ☐ I need to fix my punctuation.	**CONVENTIONS** ☐ I use correct spelling. ☐ I use correct grammar. ☐ I use correct punctuation.

Vocabulary Definitions

barn: a building on a farm for crops or animals

beaver: a busy animal with sharp teeth that lives near water

bee: an insect that makes honey

bottle: a container with a cap that a drink comes in

bristles: stiff hairs

broken: in pieces; not whole

burrow: a hole underground

bury: to put something underground

carve: to cut rock or wood to shape it into an object

cell: a small part of a hive

chimpanzee: a wild animal from Africa

claws: sharp toes on the feet of birds that hunt

cold: an illness that causes a stuffy, runny nose

Constitution: the laws and rights of a country

cough: a tickle in the throat

country: a large piece of land

court: a place where judges make sure laws are used fairly

dairy foods: milk and foods made from milk, such as cheese, yogurt, and ice cream

dam: something that stops water from moving

doctor: someone who cares for sick people

drink: to take in a liquid and swallow it

Earth: the planet we live on

earthworm: a worm that lives underground

Vocabulary Definitions, *continued*

feathers: soft parts on a bird's body, wings, legs, and face

firefighter: someone who puts out fires

flag: a cloth with a design that stands for a place

forest: woods; a place with a lot of trees

fresh water: water without salt in it

garbage: trash

garden: a place with plants in soil

germs: things that make you feel sick

growing: getting bigger

hive: a bee's home

honeycomb: many cells together

kernel: the part of a wheat plant used to make flour

lake: a large body of water with land all around

landfill: a place where trash is dumped and covered up

language: words we use to talk to each other

lawyer: someone who studies laws and helps people in court

lodge: a beaver home made of sticks, grass, and mud in a stream

map: a drawing showing where things are

milk: a white drink

mountain: a really high hill

nest: a home that some birds make to live in or lay eggs

nurse: someone who helps doctors take care of sick people

ocean: a very large body of water between continents

Vocabulary Definitions, *continued*

owls: large birds that have large heads and hunt for food

people: men, women, and children

police officer: someone who helps keep people safe

pond: a small lake

postal worker: someone who helps deliver mail

salt water: water with salt in it, mostly in oceans

school: a place where people learn

segment: a short piece

segregation: keeping different kinds of people apart

sneeze: a tickle in the nose

stalk: the long, thin part of a plant

stream: a small river

team: a group of people who play or work together

trail: a path; a place to walk

wax: what hives are made of

wheat: a plant grown to make flour

wing: the part of birds that lets them fly

workers: people who do work

UNIT 1

Geography Article – Level J
Compare-and-Contrast Writing Prompt

Lakes and Oceans

Lesson Objectives

Writing
Students use information from the geography article to write a compare-and-contrast paragraph.

Vocabulary
Students learn content vocabulary words and use those words to write about how lakes and oceans are alike and different.

Content Knowledge
Students understand that lakes and oceans are large bodies of water on Earth.

Essential Understanding
Students understand that oceans and lakes are different sizes and have different types of water.

Prepare

Reproduce and distribute one copy for each student.

LESSON		PAGE
1	Unit Focus and Lesson Checklist	12
2	Learn Vocabulary	13
3	Read the Geography Article: *Lakes and Oceans*	14
4	Answer Questions About the Geography Article	15
5	Organize Information	16
6	Write a Compare-and-Contrast Paragraph	17

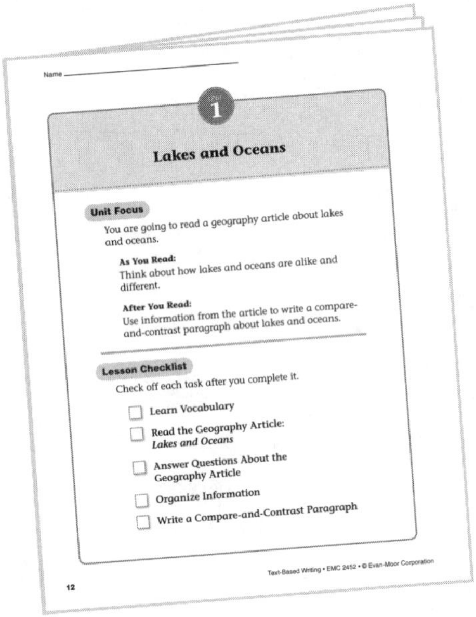
Name

Unit 1

Lakes and Oceans

Unit Focus
You are going to read a geography article about lakes and oceans.
As You Read:
Think about how lakes and oceans are alike and different.
After You Read:
Use information from the article to write a compare-and-contrast paragraph about lakes and oceans.

Lesson Checklist
Check off each task after you complete it.
☐ Learn Vocabulary
☐ Read the Geography Article: *Lakes and Oceans*
☐ Answer Questions About the Geography Article
☐ Organize Information
☐ Write a Compare-and-Contrast Paragraph

12 Text-Based Writing • EMC 2452 • © Evan-Moor Corporation

1 Unit Focus and Lesson Checklist

Distribute one unit to each student and direct students' attention to the Unit Focus and Lesson Checklist. Tell them they will be able to refer to the focus of the unit as needed while working on the lessons. Instruct students to check off each task on the checklist after they complete it.

Read aloud the focus statements, and verify that students understand their purpose for reading. Ask:

- *What are we going to read about?* (lakes and oceans)
- *What are you going to learn about them?* (how they are alike and different)
- *What are you going to write based on this article?* (a compare-and-contrast paragraph)

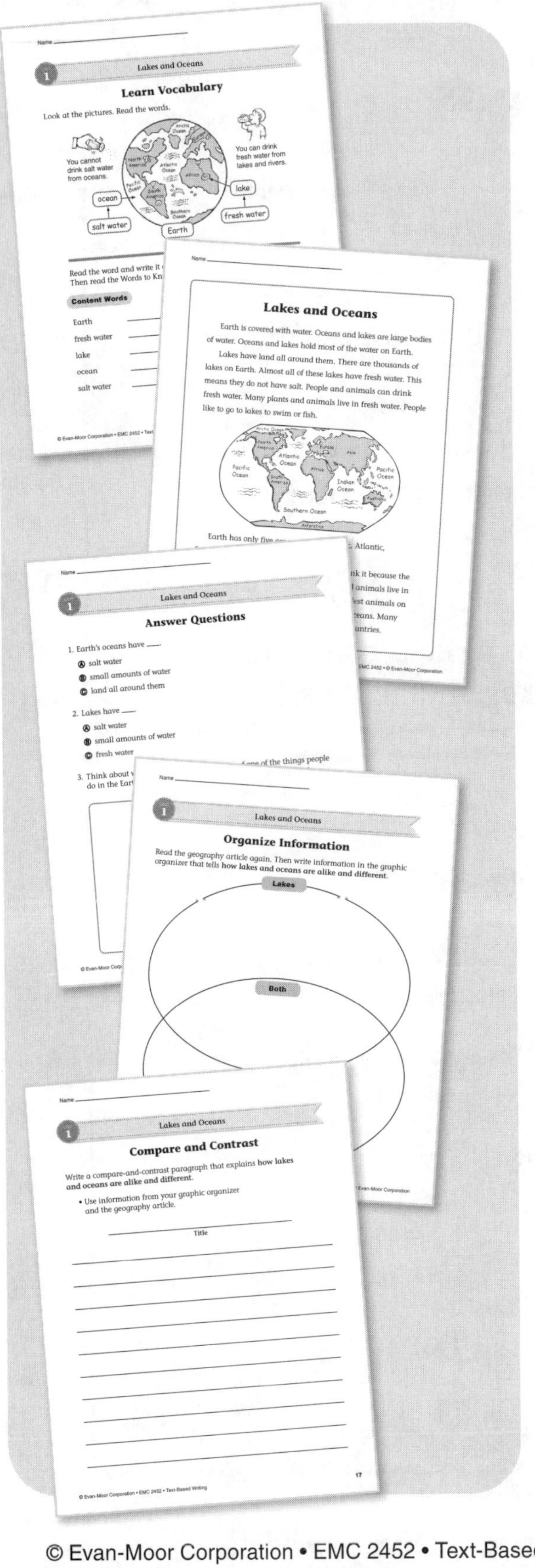

2 Learn Vocabulary

Direct students' attention to the picture dictionary. Read aloud each content vocabulary word and have students repeat. Point out that the words are related to Earth's water and that students will have a better understanding of the words after they read the geography article. Have students write the vocabulary words on the provided lines. Then review the Words to Know, and encourage students to ask questions about any words they do not understand.

3 Read the Geography Article: *Lakes and Oceans*

Read aloud the geography article as students follow along silently. Then have students reread the article independently or in small groups.

4 Answer Questions About the Geography Article

To ensure reading comprehension, have students answer the text-dependent questions. Review the answers together.

5 Organize Information

Explain to students that they will use a compare-and-contrast graphic organizer to help them plan their paragraphs. Guide students in using the text to complete the organizer, rereading the article if needed.

Remind students that a compare-and-contrast paragraph:

- tells how two or more things are alike, and
- tells how two or more things are different.

6 Write a Compare-and-Contrast Paragraph

Instruct students to complete the writing assignment independently, with a partner, or in small groups.

If needed, review the structure of a compare-and-contrast paragraph:

- The topic sentence tells about the two subjects.
- Details tell how the subjects are alike and different.

Name ___________________________

UNIT 1

Lakes and Oceans

Unit Focus

You are going to read a geography article about lakes and oceans.

As You Read:
Think about how lakes and oceans are alike and different.

After You Read:
Use information from the article to write a compare-and-contrast paragraph about lakes and oceans.

Lesson Checklist

Check off each task after you complete it.

- ☐ **Learn Vocabulary**
- ☐ **Read the Geography Article: *Lakes and Oceans***
- ☐ **Answer Questions About the Geography Article**
- ☐ **Organize Information**
- ☐ **Write a Compare-and-Contrast Paragraph**

Name ___________________________

UNIT 1

Lakes and Oceans

Learn Vocabulary

Look at the pictures. Read the words.

You cannot drink salt water from oceans.

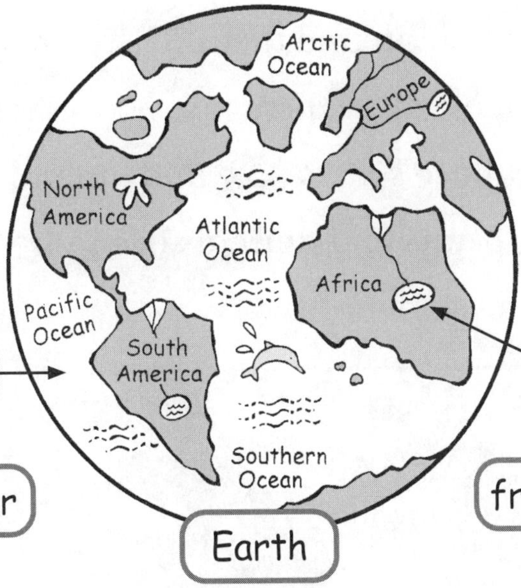

You can drink fresh water from lakes and rivers.

Read the word and write it on the line.
Then read the Words to Know.

Content Words

Earth ___________________

fresh water ___________________

lake ___________________

ocean ___________________

salt water ___________________

Words to Know

bodies
planet
countries
swim
fish

Name ____________________

Lakes and Oceans

Earth is covered with water. Oceans and lakes are large bodies of water. Oceans and lakes hold most of the water on Earth.

Lakes have land all around them. There are thousands of lakes on Earth. Almost all of these lakes have fresh water. This means they do not have salt. People and animals can drink fresh water. Many plants and animals live in fresh water. People like to go to lakes to swim or fish.

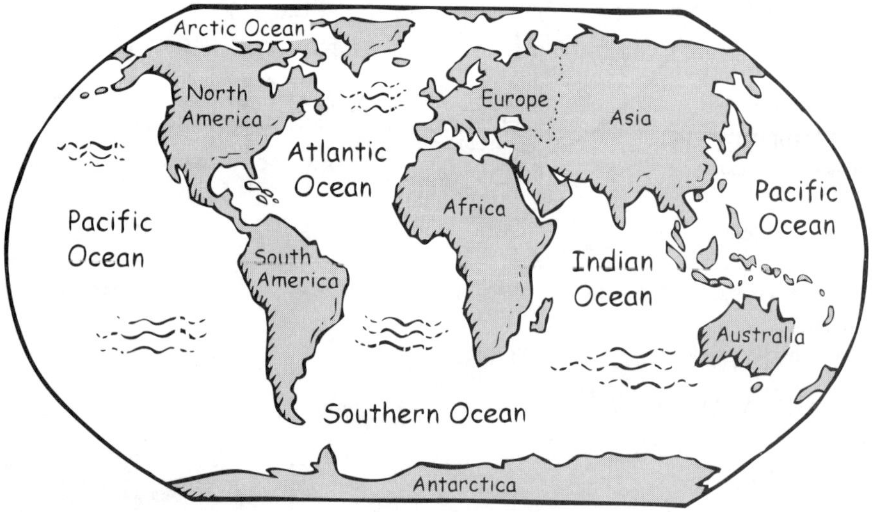

Earth has only five oceans: Arctic, Pacific, Atlantic, Southern, and Indian.

Oceans have salt water. People cannot drink it because the salt will make them sick. But many plants and animals live in oceans. They are some of the largest and smallest animals on the planet. Many fishermen go fishing in the oceans. Many people travel across oceans to get to different countries.

Name ______________________________

UNIT 1 Lakes and Oceans

Answer Questions

1. Earth's oceans have ____.

Ⓐ salt water

Ⓑ small amounts of water

Ⓒ land all around them

2. Lakes have ____.

Ⓐ salt water

Ⓑ small amounts of water

Ⓒ fresh water

3. Think about what you read. Draw a picture of one of the things people do in the Earth's oceans. Write a sentence to go with your picture.

Name ___________________________________

UNIT 1

Lakes and Oceans

Organize Information

Read the geography article again. Then write information in the graphic organizer that tells **how lakes and oceans are alike and different.**

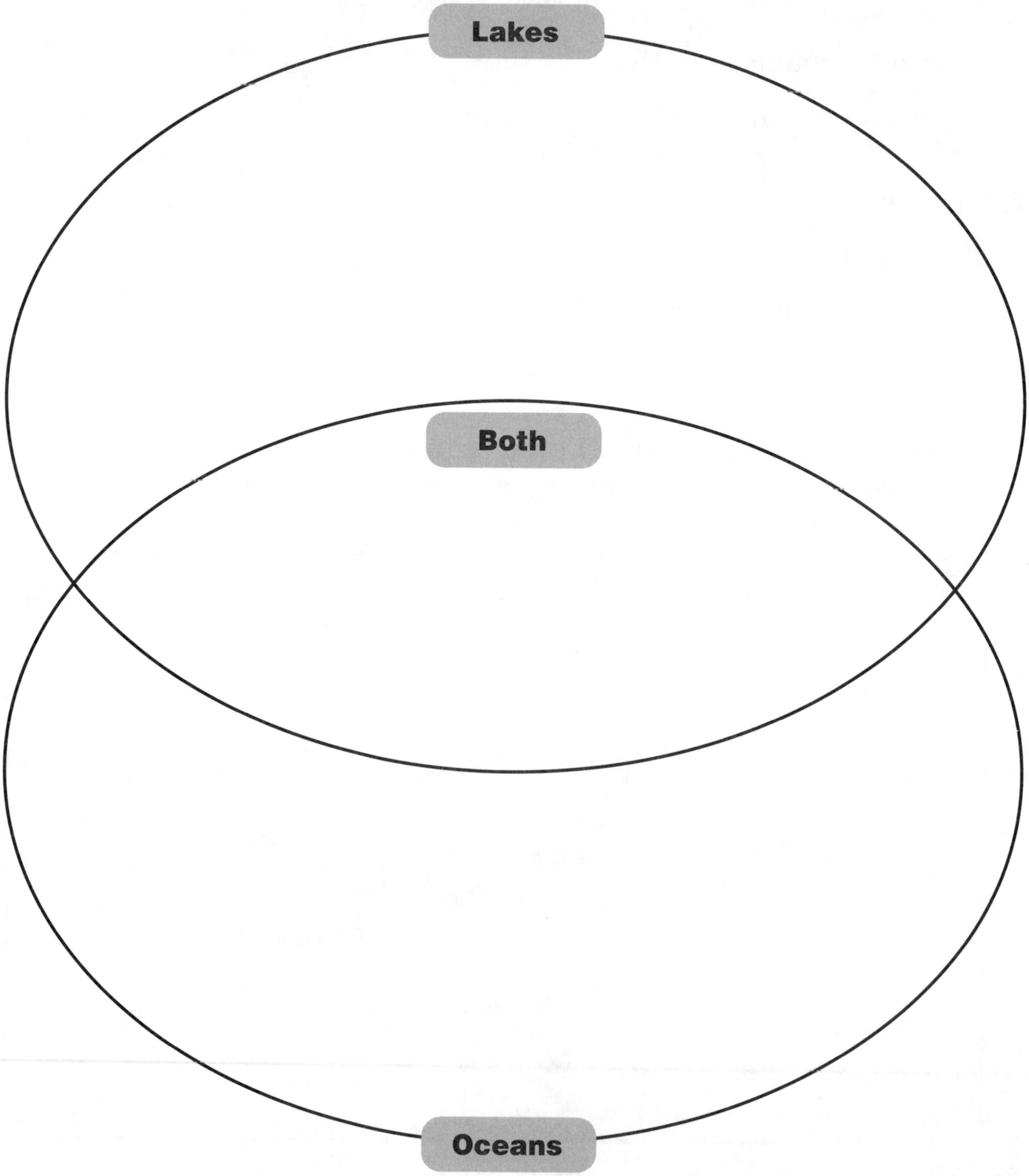

Name ____________________

UNIT 1 Lakes and Oceans

Compare and Contrast

Write a compare-and-contrast paragraph that explains **how lakes and oceans are alike and different.**

- Use information from your graphic organizer and the geography article.

____

Title

UNIT 2

Science Article – Level L

Compare-and-Contrast Writing Prompt

Owl Facts

Lesson Objectives

Writing

Students use information from the science article to write a compare-and-contrast paragraph.

Vocabulary

Students learn content vocabulary words and use those words to write about how owls are alike and different.

Content Knowledge

Students understand the unique characteristics of snowy owls and barn owls.

Essential Understanding

Students understand what owls look like and how they live and act in nature.

Prepare

Reproduce and distribute one copy for each student.

LESSON		PAGE
1	Unit Focus and Lesson Checklist	20
2	Learn Vocabulary	21
3	Read the Science Article: *Owl Facts*	22
4	Answer Questions About the Science Article	23
5	Organize Information	24
6	Write a Compare-and-Contrast Paragraph	25

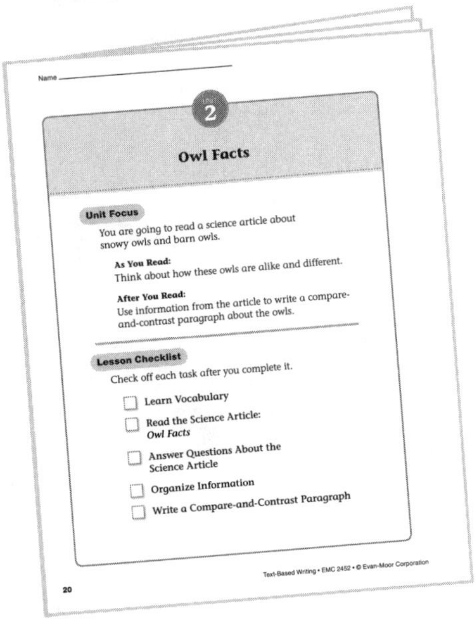
Name

2

Owl Facts

Unit Focus

You are going to read a science article about snowy owls and barn owls.

As You Read:
Think about how these owls are alike and different.

After You Read:
Use information from the article to write a compare-and-contrast paragraph about the owls.

Lesson Checklist

Check off each task after you complete it.

- [ ] Learn Vocabulary
- [ ] Read the Science Article: *Owl Facts*
- [ ] Answer Questions About the Science Article
- [ ] Organize Information
- [ ] Write a Compare-and-Contrast Paragraph

20 Text-Based Writing • EMC 2452 • © Evan-Moor Corporation

1 Unit Focus and Lesson Checklist

Distribute one unit to each student and direct students' attention to the Unit Focus and Lesson Checklist. Tell them they will be able to refer to the focus of the unit as needed while working on the lessons. Instruct students to check off each task on the checklist after they complete it.

Read aloud the focus statements, and verify that students understand their purpose for reading. Ask:

- *What are we going to read about?* (snowy owls and barn owls)
- *What are you going to learn about them?* (how they are alike and different)
- *What are you going to write based on this article?* (a compare-and-contrast paragraph)

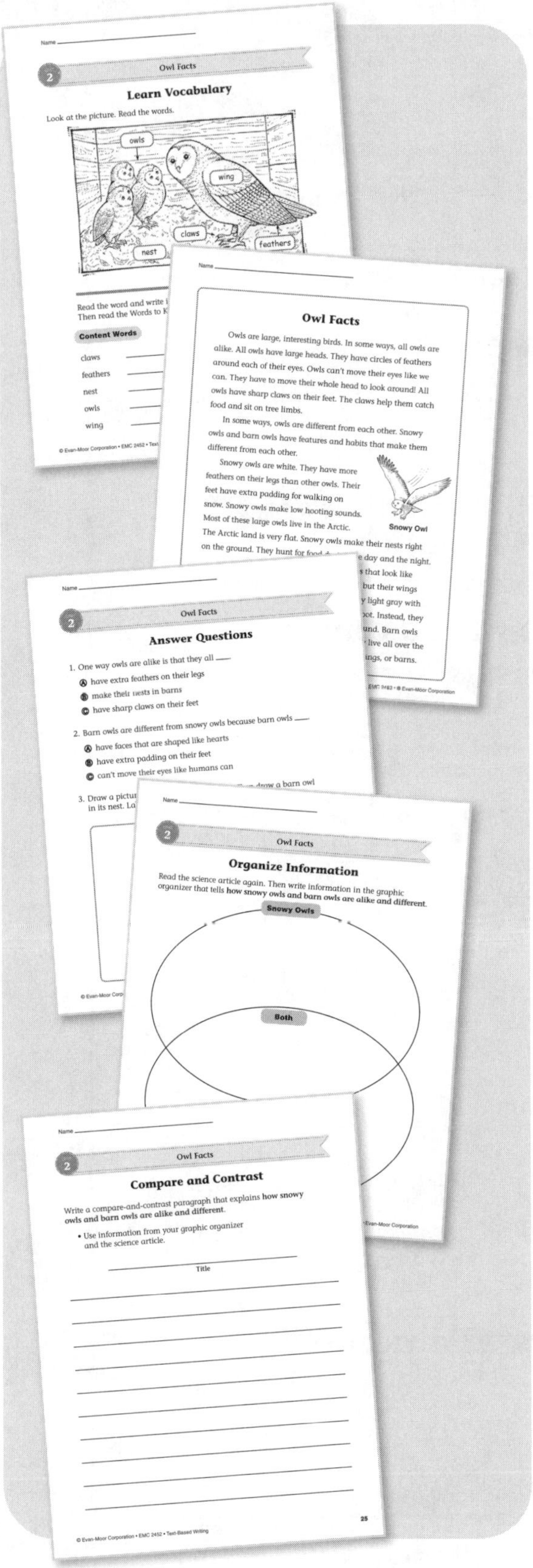

2 Learn Vocabulary

Direct students' attention to the picture dictionary. Read aloud each content vocabulary word and have students repeat. Point out that the words are related to owls and that students will have a better understanding of the words after they read the science article. Have students write the vocabulary words on the provided lines. Then review the Words to Know, and encourage students to ask questions about any words they do not understand.

3 Read the Science Article: *Owl Facts*

Read aloud the science article as students follow along silently. Then have students reread the article independently or in small groups.

4 Answer Questions About the Science Article

To ensure reading comprehension, have students answer the text-dependent questions. Review the answers together.

5 Organize Information

Explain to students that they will use a compare-and-contrast graphic organizer to help them plan their paragraphs. Guide students in using the text to complete the organizer, rereading the article if needed.

Remind students that a compare-and-contrast paragraph:

- tells how two or more things are alike, and
- tells how two or more things are different.

6 Write a Compare-and-Contrast Paragraph

Instruct students to complete the writing assignment independently, with a partner, or in small groups.

If needed, review the structure of a compare-and-contrast paragraph:

- The topic sentence tells about the two subjects.
- Details support the topic sentence and tell how the subjects are alike and different.

Name ______________________________

UNIT 2

Owl Facts

Unit Focus

You are going to read a science article about snowy owls and barn owls.

As You Read:
Think about how these owls are alike and different.

After You Read:
Use information from the article to write a compare-and-contrast paragraph about the owls.

Lesson Checklist

Check off each task after you complete it.

- ☐ **Learn Vocabulary**
- ☐ **Read the Science Article: *Owl Facts***
- ☐ **Answer Questions About the Science Article**
- ☐ **Organize Information**
- ☐ **Write a Compare-and-Contrast Paragraph**

Name ________________________________

UNIT 2 Owl Facts

Learn Vocabulary

Look at the picture. Read the words.

Read the word and write it on the line.
Then read the Words to Know.

Content Words

claws ____________________

feathers ____________________

nest ____________________

owls ____________________

wing ____________________

Words to Know

Arctic	hiss
eyes	hoot
habits	interesting
heads	screech

Name ____

Owl Facts

Owls are large, interesting birds. In some ways, all owls are alike. All owls have large heads. They have circles of feathers around each of their eyes. Owls can't move their eyes like we can. They have to move their whole head to look around! All owls have sharp claws on their feet. The claws help them catch food and sit on tree limbs.

In some ways, owls are different from each other. Snowy owls and barn owls have features and habits that make them different from each other.

Snowy Owl

Snowy owls are white. They have more feathers on their legs than other owls. Their feet have extra padding for walking on snow. Snowy owls make low hooting sounds. Most of these large owls live in the Arctic. The Arctic land is very flat. Snowy owls make their nests right on the ground. They hunt for food during the day and the night.

Barn Owl

Barn owls have white faces that look like hearts. Their bodies are small, but their wings are large. Barn owls are usually light gray with some spots. Barn owls do not hoot. Instead, they make a hissing or screeching sound. Barn owls hunt for food only at night. They live all over the world. They make their nests in tree holes, buildings, or barns.

Name ______________________________

UNIT 2

Owl Facts

Answer Questions

1. One way owls are alike is that they all ___.

   Ⓐ have extra feathers on their legs

   Ⓑ make their nests in barns

   Ⓒ have sharp claws on their feet

2. Barn owls are different from snowy owls because barn owls ___.

   Ⓐ have faces that are shaped like hearts

   Ⓑ have extra padding on their feet

   Ⓒ can't move their eyes like humans can

3. Draw a picture of a snowy owl in its nest. Then draw a barn owl in its nest. Label each part of your pictures.

Name ______________________________

UNIT 2 **Owl Facts**

Organize Information

Read the science article again. Then write information in the graphic organizer that tells **how snowy owls and barn owls are alike and different.**

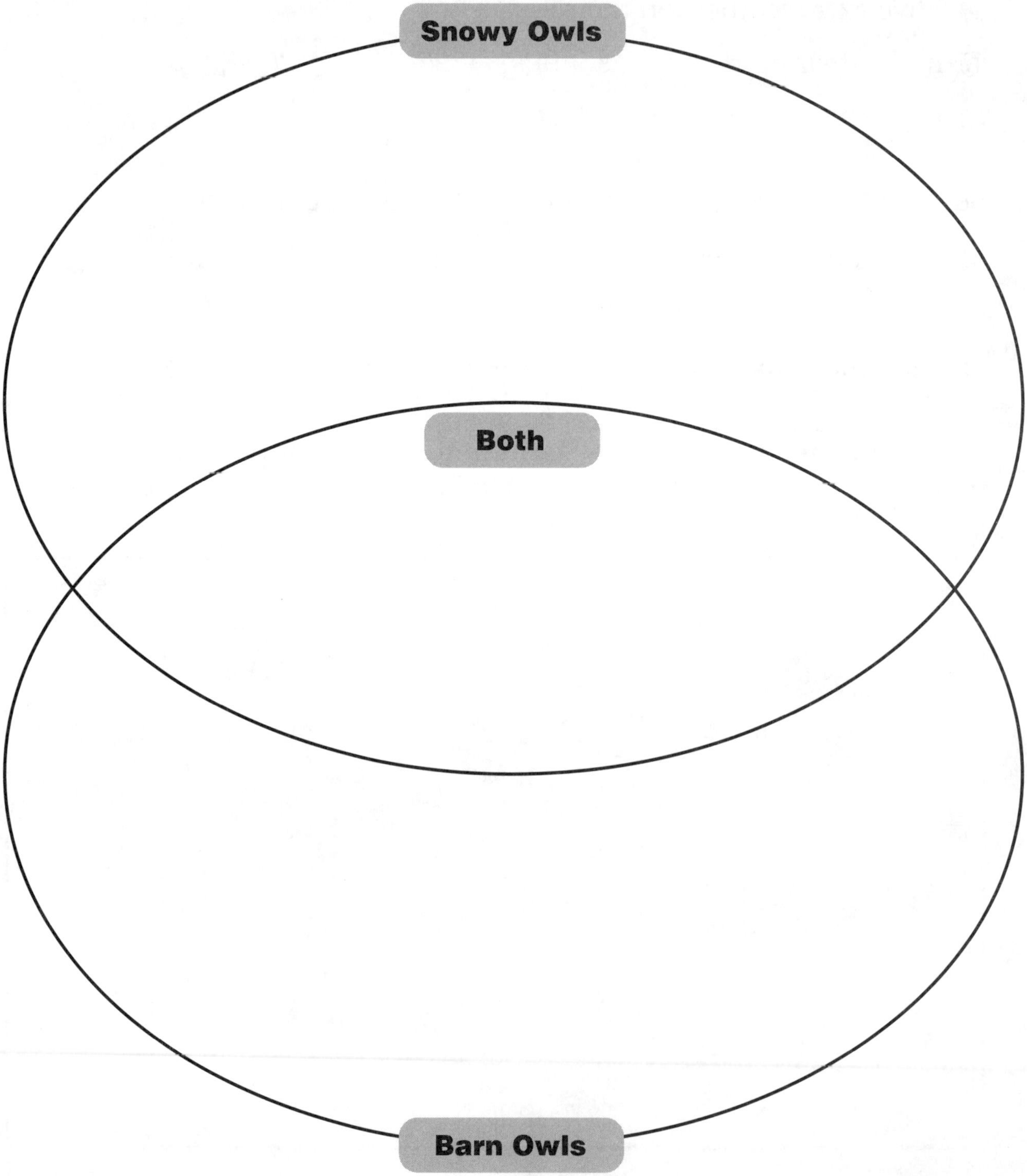

Name ______________________________

UNIT 2 Owl Facts

Compare and Contrast

Write a compare-and-contrast paragraph that explains **how snowy owls and barn owls are alike and different**.

- Use information from your graphic organizer and the science article.

____

Title

Beavers at Work

Lesson Objectives

Writing
Students use information from the science article to write a sequence paragraph.

Vocabulary
Students learn content vocabulary words and use those words to tell how beavers make and use lodges.

Content Knowledge
Students understand that beavers use their bodies and environments to build unique homes.

Essential Understanding
Students understand that some animals, such as beavers, are built to naturally perform certain tasks.

Prepare

Reproduce and distribute one copy for each student.

LESSON		PAGE
1	Unit Focus and Lesson Checklist	**28**
2	Learn Vocabulary	**29**
3	Read the Science Article: *Beavers at Work*	**30**
4	Answer Questions About the Science Article	**31**
5	Organize Information	**32**
6	Write a Sequence Paragraph	**33**

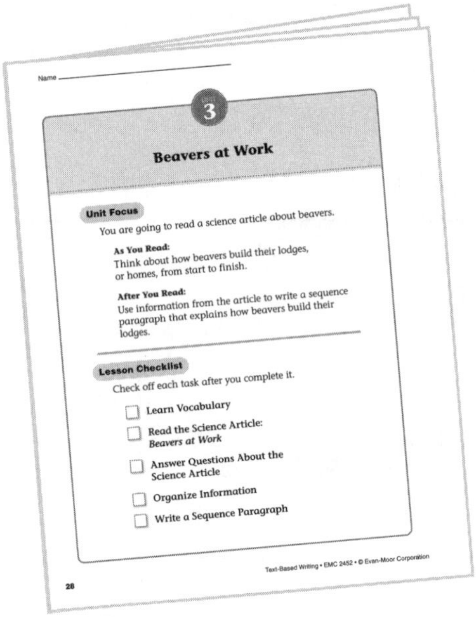
Name

3

Beavers at Work

Unit Focus
You are going to read a science article about beavers.

As You Read:
Think about how beavers build their lodges, or homes, from start to finish.

After You Read:
Use information from the article to write a sequence paragraph that explains how beavers build their lodges.

Lesson Checklist
Check off each task after you complete it.

- [ ] Learn Vocabulary
- [ ] Read the Science Article: *Beavers at Work*
- [ ] Answer Questions About the Science Article
- [ ] Organize Information
- [ ] Write a Sequence Paragraph

28 Text-Based Writing • EMC 2452 • © Evan-Moor Corporation

1 Unit Focus and Lesson Checklist

Distribute one unit to each student and direct students' attention to the Unit Focus and Lesson Checklist. Tell them they will be able to refer to the focus of the unit as needed while working on the lessons. Instruct students to check off each task on the checklist after they complete it.

Read aloud the focus statements, and verify that students understand their purpose for reading. Ask:

- *What are we going to read about?* (beavers)
- *What are you going to learn about beavers?* (how they build lodges)
- *What are you going to write based on this article?* (a sequence paragraph)

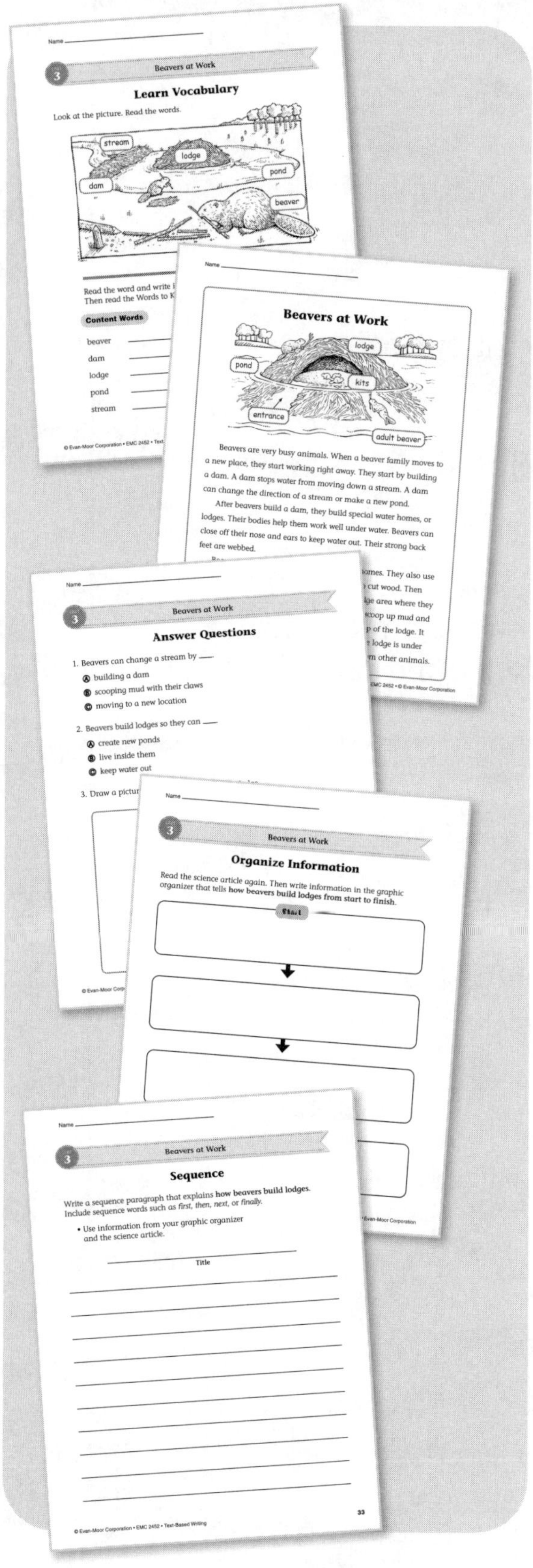

2 **Learn Vocabulary**
Direct students' attention to the picture dictionary. Read aloud each content vocabulary word and have students repeat. Point out that the words are related to beavers and that students will have a better understanding of the words after they read the science article. Have students write the vocabulary words on the provided lines. Then review the Words to Know, and encourage students to ask questions about any words they do not understand.

3 **Read the Science Article: *Beavers at Work***
Read aloud the science article. Then have students reread the article independently or in small groups.

4 **Answer Questions About the Science Article**
To ensure reading comprehension, have students answer the text-dependent questions. Review the answers together.

5 **Organize Information**
Explain to students that they will use a sequence graphic organizer to help them plan their paragraphs. Guide students in using the text to complete the organizer, rereading the article if needed.

Remind students that a sequence paragraph:

- tells the chronological order, or time order, of events, and
- allows readers to understand exactly how a process works.

6 **Write a Sequence Paragraph**
Instruct students to complete the writing assignment independently, with a partner, or in small groups.

If needed, review the structure of a sequence paragraph:

- The topic sentence tells the subject of the paragraph.
- Detail sentences support the topic sentence and list the events or steps in order.

Name ________________________________

UNIT 3

Beavers at Work

Unit Focus

You are going to read a science article about beavers.

As You Read:
Think about how beavers build their lodges, or homes, from start to finish.

After You Read:
Use information from the article to write a sequence paragraph that explains how beavers build their lodges.

Lesson Checklist

Check off each task after you complete it.

- ☐ **Learn Vocabulary**
- ☐ **Read the Science Article: *Beavers at Work***
- ☐ **Answer Questions About the Science Article**
- ☐ **Organize Information**
- ☐ **Write a Sequence Paragraph**

Name ___________________________________

UNIT 3 Beavers at Work

Learn Vocabulary

Look at the picture. Read the words.

Read the word and write it on the line.
Then read the Words to Know.

Content Words

beaver ______________________

dam ______________________

lodge ______________________

pond ______________________

stream ______________________

Words to Know

building	scoop
claws	sharp
direction	webbed
entrance	working

Name ___________________________________

Beavers at Work

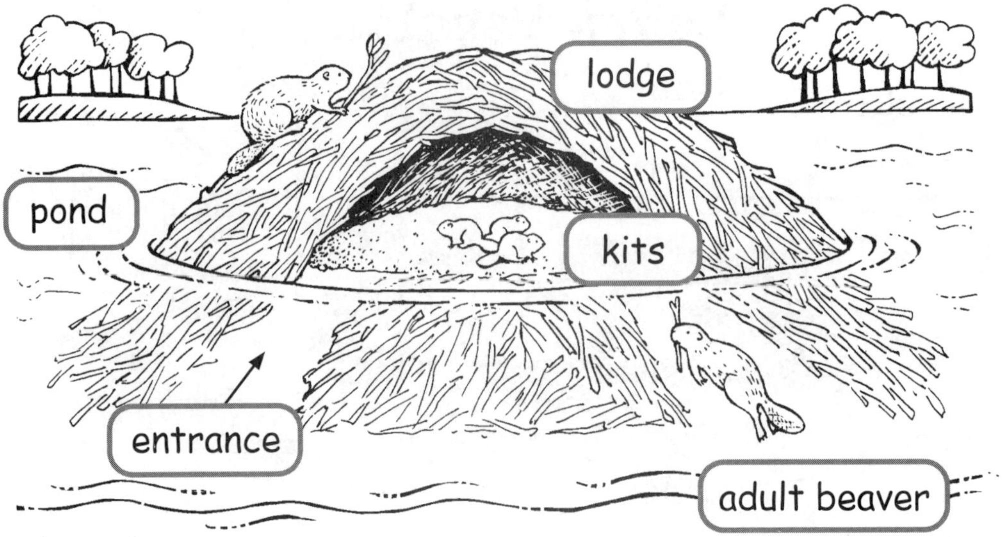

Beavers are very busy animals. When a beaver family moves to a new place, they start working right away. They start by building a dam. A dam stops water from moving down a stream. A dam can change the direction of a stream or make a new pond.

After beavers build a dam, they build special water homes, or lodges. Their bodies help them work well under water. Beavers can close off their nose and ears to keep water out. Their strong back feet are webbed.

Beavers use sticks and grass to build their homes. They also use mud. First, beavers use their sharp front teeth to cut wood. Then they push the wood through the water to the lodge area where they stack the wood. Next, beavers use their claws to scoop up mud and grass. Finally, they pack the mud and grass on top of the lodge. It holds all of the sticks together. The entrance to the lodge is under the water. Beaver lodges help keep beavers safe from other animals.

Name ____________________

UNIT 3

Beavers at Work

Answer Questions

1. Beavers can change a stream by ____.

   Ⓐ building a dam

   Ⓑ scooping mud with their claws

   Ⓒ moving to a new location

2. Beavers build lodges so they can ____.

   Ⓐ create new ponds

   Ⓑ live inside them

   Ⓒ keep water out

3. Draw a picture of a beaver working on its lodge.

Name ______________________________

UNIT 3 Beavers at Work

Organize Information

Read the science article again. Then write information in the graphic organizer that tells **how beavers build lodges from start to finish**.

Start

↓

↓

↓

Finish

Name ____________________

UNIT 3

Beavers at Work

Sequence

Write a sequence paragraph that explains **how beavers build lodges.** Include sequence words such as *first, then, next,* or *finally.*

- Use information from your graphic organizer and the science article.

____

Title

____

____

____

____

____

____

____

____

____

____

UNIT 4

Science Article – Level M

Sequence Writing Prompt

The Life of a Worker Bee

Lesson Objectives

Writing
Students use information from the science article to write a sequence paragraph.

Vocabulary
Students learn content vocabulary words and use those words to write about worker bees.

Content Knowledge
Students understand that worker bees perform different jobs as they grow.

Essential Understanding
Students understand that some creatures, such as bees, focus primarily on how to help their group rather than just themselves.

Prepare

Reproduce and distribute one copy for each student.

LESSON		PAGE
1	Unit Focus and Lesson Checklist	**36**
2	Learn Vocabulary	**37**
3	Read the Science Article: *The Life of a Worker Bee*	**38**
4	Answer Questions About the Science Article	**39**
5	Organize Information	**40**
6	Write a Sequence Paragraph	**41**

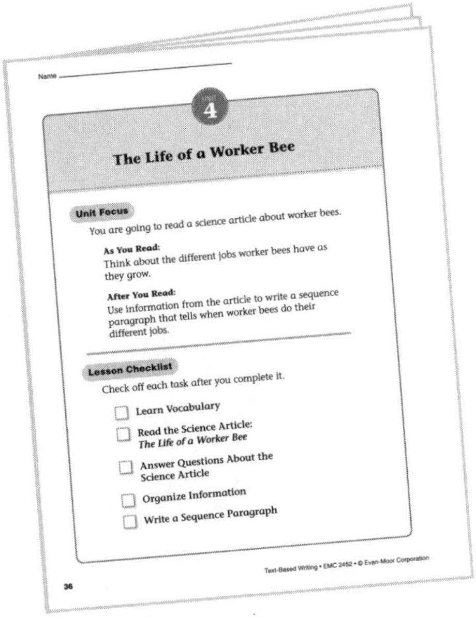
Name

UNIT 4

The Life of a Worker Bee

Unit Focus

You are going to read a science article about worker bees.

As You Read:
Think about the different jobs worker bees have as they grow.

After You Read:
Use information from the article to write a sequence paragraph that tells when worker bees do their different jobs.

Lesson Checklist

Check off each task after you complete it.

- ☐ Learn Vocabulary
- ☐ Read the Science Article: *The Life of a Worker Bee*
- ☐ Answer Questions About the Science Article
- ☐ Organize Information
- ☐ Write a Sequence Paragraph

36

Text-Based Writing • EMC 2452 • © Evan-Moor Corporation

1 Unit Focus and Lesson Checklist

Distribute one unit to each student and direct students' attention to the Unit Focus and Lesson Checklist. Tell them they will be able to refer to the focus of the unit as needed while working on the lessons. Instruct students to check off each task on the checklist after they complete it.

Read aloud the focus statements, and verify that students understand their purpose for reading. Ask:

- *What are we going to read about?* (worker bees)
- *What are you going to learn about worker bees?* (what jobs they do in their lifetime)
- *What are you going to write based on this article?* (a sequence paragraph)

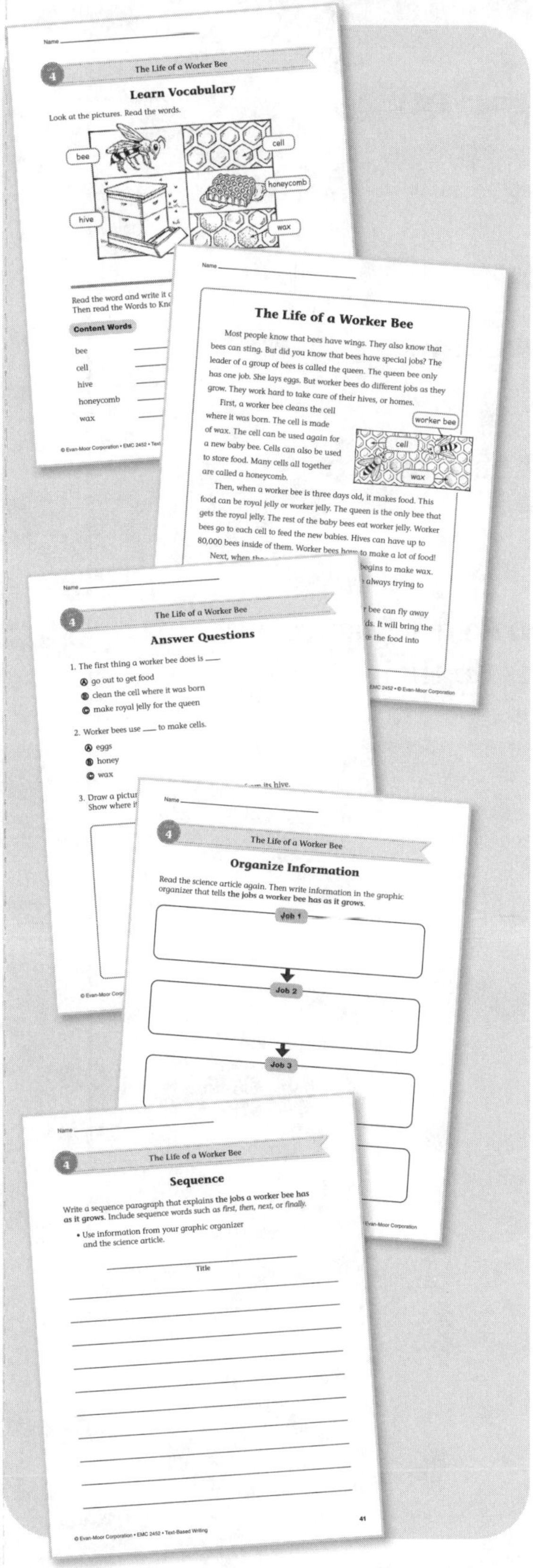

2 Learn Vocabulary

Direct students' attention to the picture dictionary. Read aloud each content vocabulary word and have students repeat. Point out that the words are related to worker bees and that students will have a better understanding of the words after they read the science article. Have students write the vocabulary words on the provided lines. Then review the Words to Know, and encourage students to ask questions about any words they do not understand.

3 Read the Science Article: *The Life of a Worker Bee*

Read aloud the science article. Then have students reread the article independently or in small groups.

4 Answer Questions About the Science Article

To ensure reading comprehension, have students answer the text-dependent questions. Review the answers together.

5 Organize Information

Explain to students that they will use a sequence graphic organizer to help them plan their paragraphs. Guide students in using the text to complete the organizer, rereading the article if needed.

Remind students that a sequence paragraph:

- tells the chronological order, or time order, of events, and
- allows readers to understand exactly how a process works.

6 Write a Sequence Paragraph

Instruct students to complete the writing assignment independently, with a partner, or in small groups.

If needed, review the structure of a sequence paragraph:

- The topic sentence tells the subject of the paragraph.
- Detail sentences support the topic sentence and list the events in order.

Name ______________________________

UNIT 4

The Life of a Worker Bee

Unit Focus

You are going to read a science article about worker bees.

As You Read:
Think about the different jobs worker bees have as they grow.

After You Read:
Use information from the article to write a sequence paragraph that tells when worker bees do their different jobs.

Lesson Checklist

Check off each task after you complete it.

- [ ] **Learn Vocabulary**
- [ ] **Read the Science Article:** ***The Life of a Worker Bee***
- [ ] **Answer Questions About the Science Article**
- [ ] **Organize Information**
- [ ] **Write a Sequence Paragraph**

Name ______________________________

UNIT 4

The Life of a Worker Bee

Learn Vocabulary

Look at the pictures. Read the words.

Read the word and write it on the line.
Then read the Words to Know.

Content Words

bee ______________________

cell ______________________

hive ______________________

honeycomb ______________________

wax ______________________

Words to Know

busy	royal
honey	special
jelly	sting
queen	worker

Name ____________________

The Life of a Worker Bee

Most people know that bees have wings. They also know that bees can sting. But did you know that bees have special jobs? The leader of a group of bees is called the queen. The queen bee only has one job. She lays eggs. But worker bees do different jobs as they grow. They work hard to take care of their hives, or homes.

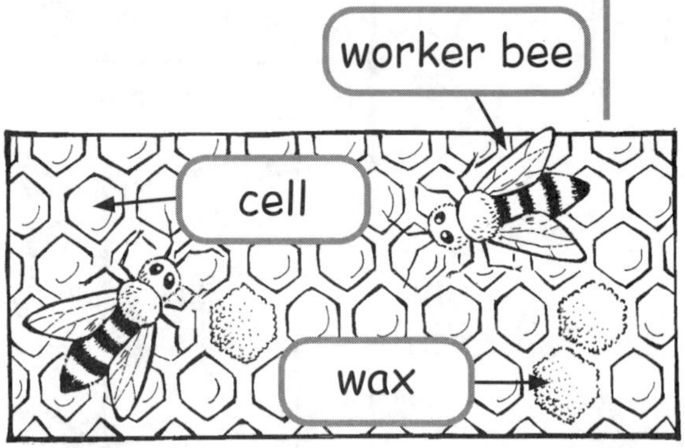

First, a worker bee cleans the cell where it was born. The cell is made of wax. The cell can be used again for a new baby bee. Cells can also be used to store food. Many cells all together are called a honeycomb.

Then, when a worker bee is three days old, it makes food. This food can be royal jelly or worker jelly. The queen is the only bee that gets the royal jelly. The rest of the baby bees eat worker jelly. Worker bees go to each cell to feed the new babies. Hives can have up to 80,000 bees inside of them. Worker bees have to make a lot of food!

Next, when the worker bee is a bit older, it begins to make wax. The wax is used to build new cells. The bees are always trying to make their hive bigger and better.

Finally, when it is three weeks old, the worker bee can fly away from the hive. It looks for food in flowers and fields. It will bring the food back to the hive. There, the workers will make the food into honey. Worker bees have a busy life!

Name ______________________________

Answer Questions

1. The first thing a worker bee does is ___.

   Ⓐ go out to get food

   Ⓑ clean the cell where it was born

   Ⓒ make royal jelly for the queen

2. Worker bees use ___ to make cells.

   Ⓐ eggs

   Ⓑ honey

   Ⓒ wax

3. Draw a picture of a worker bee flying away from its hive. Show where it is going.

Name ___________________________________

UNIT 4 The Life of a Worker Bee

Organize Information

Read the science article again. Then write information in the graphic organizer that tells **the jobs a worker bee has as it grows.**

Job 1

Job 2

Job 3

Job 4

Name ____________________

UNIT 4

The Life of a Worker Bee

Sequence

Write a sequence paragraph that explains **the jobs a worker bee has as it grows**. Include sequence words such as *first, then, next,* or *finally.*

- Use information from your graphic organizer and the science article.

____

Title

Community Helpers

Lesson Objectives

Writing
Students use information from the social studies article to write an explanatory paragraph.

Vocabulary
Students learn content vocabulary words and use those words to write about the people who work in their community.

Content Knowledge
Students understand that community helpers perform specific tasks.

Essential Understanding
Students understand that communities need these types of helpers to stay productive and safe.

Prepare

Reproduce and distribute one copy for each student.

LESSON		PAGE
1	Unit Focus and Lesson Checklist	44
2	Learn Vocabulary	45
3	Read the Social Studies Article: *Community Helpers*	46
4	Answer Questions About the Social Studies Article	47
5	Organize Information	48
6	Write an Explanatory Paragraph	49

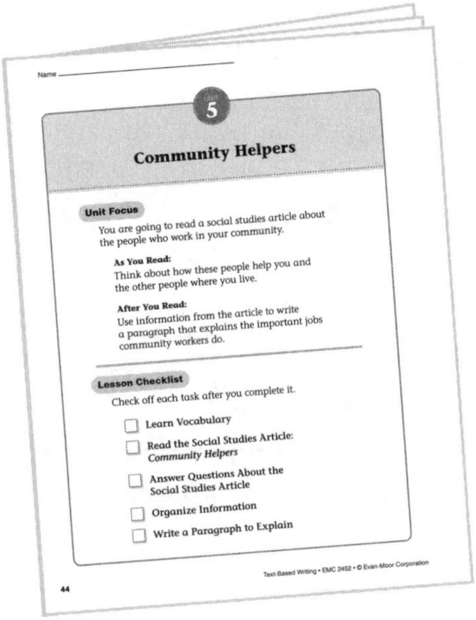
Name

5

Community Helpers

Unit Focus
You are going to read a social studies article about the people who work in your community.

As You Read:
Think about how these people help you and the other people where you live.

After You Read:
Use information from the article to write a paragraph that explains the important jobs community workers do.

Lesson Checklist
Check off each task after you complete it.

- ☐ Learn Vocabulary
- ☐ Read the Social Studies Article: *Community Helpers*
- ☐ Answer Questions About the Social Studies Article
- ☐ Organize Information
- ☐ Write a Paragraph to Explain

44 Text-Based Writing • EMC 2452 • © Evan-Moor Corporation

1 Unit Focus and Lesson Checklist

Distribute one unit to each student and direct students' attention to the Unit Focus and Lesson Checklist. Tell them they will be able to refer to the focus of the unit as needed while working on the lessons. Instruct students to check off each task on the checklist after they complete it.

Read aloud the focus statements, and verify that students understand their purpose for reading. Ask:

- *What are we going to read about?* (community helpers)
- *What are you going to learn about them?* (how they help others)
- *What are you going to write based on this article?* (a paragraph that explains)

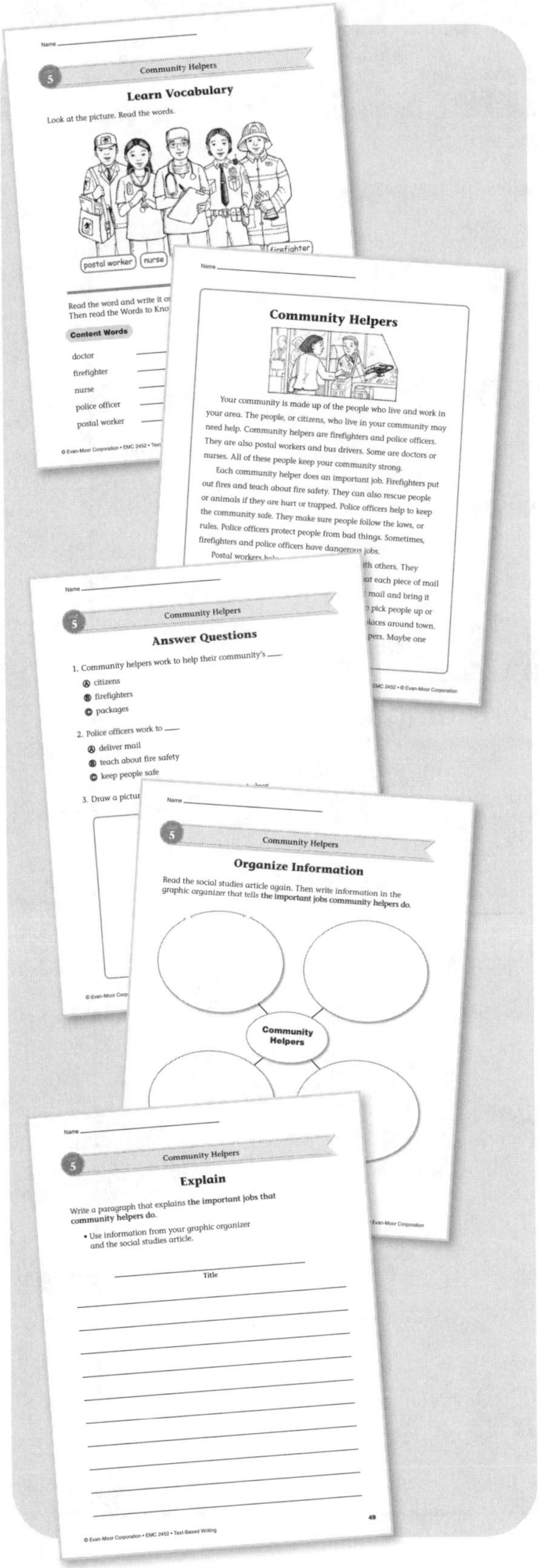

2 Learn Vocabulary

Direct students' attention to the picture dictionary. Read aloud each content vocabulary word and have students repeat. Point out that the words are related to community helpers and that students will have a better understanding of the words after they read the social studies article. Have students write the vocabulary words on the provided lines. Then review the Words to Know, and encourage students to ask questions about any words they do not understand.

3 Read the Social Studies Article: *Community Helpers*

Read aloud the social studies article as students follow along silently. Then have students reread the article independently or in small groups.

4 Answer Questions About the Social Studies Article

To ensure reading comprehension, have students answer the text-dependent questions. Review the answers together.

5 Organize Information

Explain to students that they will use an idea-web graphic organizer to help them plan their paragraphs. Guide students in using the text to complete the organizer, rereading the article if needed.

Remind students that a paragraph that explains:

- tells why something is important, or
- tells why or how something works.

6 Write an Explanatory Paragraph

Instruct students to complete the writing assignment independently, with a partner, or in small groups.

If needed, review the structure of an explanatory paragraph:

- The topic sentence introduces the subject.
- Detail sentences explain the topic to the reader.

Name ____________________________________

UNIT
5

Community Helpers

Unit Focus

You are going to read a social studies article about the people who work in your community.

As You Read:
Think about how these people help you and the other people where you live.

After You Read:
Use information from the article to write a paragraph that explains the important jobs community workers do.

Lesson Checklist

Check off each task after you complete it.

- ☐ Learn Vocabulary
- ☐ Read the Social Studies Article: *Community Helpers*
- ☐ Answer Questions About the Social Studies Article
- ☐ Organize Information
- ☐ Write a Paragraph to Explain

Name ______________________________

UNIT 5

Community Helpers

Learn Vocabulary

Look at the picture. Read the words.

Read the word and write it on the line.
Then read the Words to Know.

Content Words

doctor ______________________

firefighter ______________________

nurse ______________________

police officer ______________________

postal worker ______________________

Words to Know

citizens	laws
collect	protect
community	rescue
dangerous	safe

Name ____________________

Community Helpers

Your community is made up of the people who live and work in your area. The people, or citizens, who live in your community may need help. Community helpers are firefighters and police officers. They are also postal workers and bus drivers. Some are doctors or nurses. All of these people keep your community strong.

Each community helper does an important job. Firefighters put out fires and teach about fire safety. They can also rescue people or animals if they are hurt or trapped. Police officers help to keep the community safe. They make sure people follow the laws, or rules. Police officers protect people from bad things. Sometimes, firefighters and police officers have dangerous jobs.

Postal workers help people keep in touch with others. They deliver letters and packages. They make sure that each piece of mail is delivered to the right person. They also collect mail and bring it to the post office. Bus drivers drive to bus stops to pick people up or drop them off. They help people get to different places around town.

Both men and women can be community helpers. Maybe one day you can be a community helper, too.

Name ___________________________

UNIT 5 Community Helpers

Answer Questions

1. Community helpers work to help their community's ___.

   Ⓐ citizens

   Ⓑ firefighters

   Ⓒ packages

2. Police officers work to ___.

   Ⓐ deliver mail

   Ⓑ teach about fire safety

   Ⓒ keep people safe

3. Draw a picture of your favorite community helper.

Name ____________________________________

UNIT 5 Community Helpers

Organize Information

Read the social studies article again. Then write information in the graphic organizer that tells **the important jobs community helpers do.**

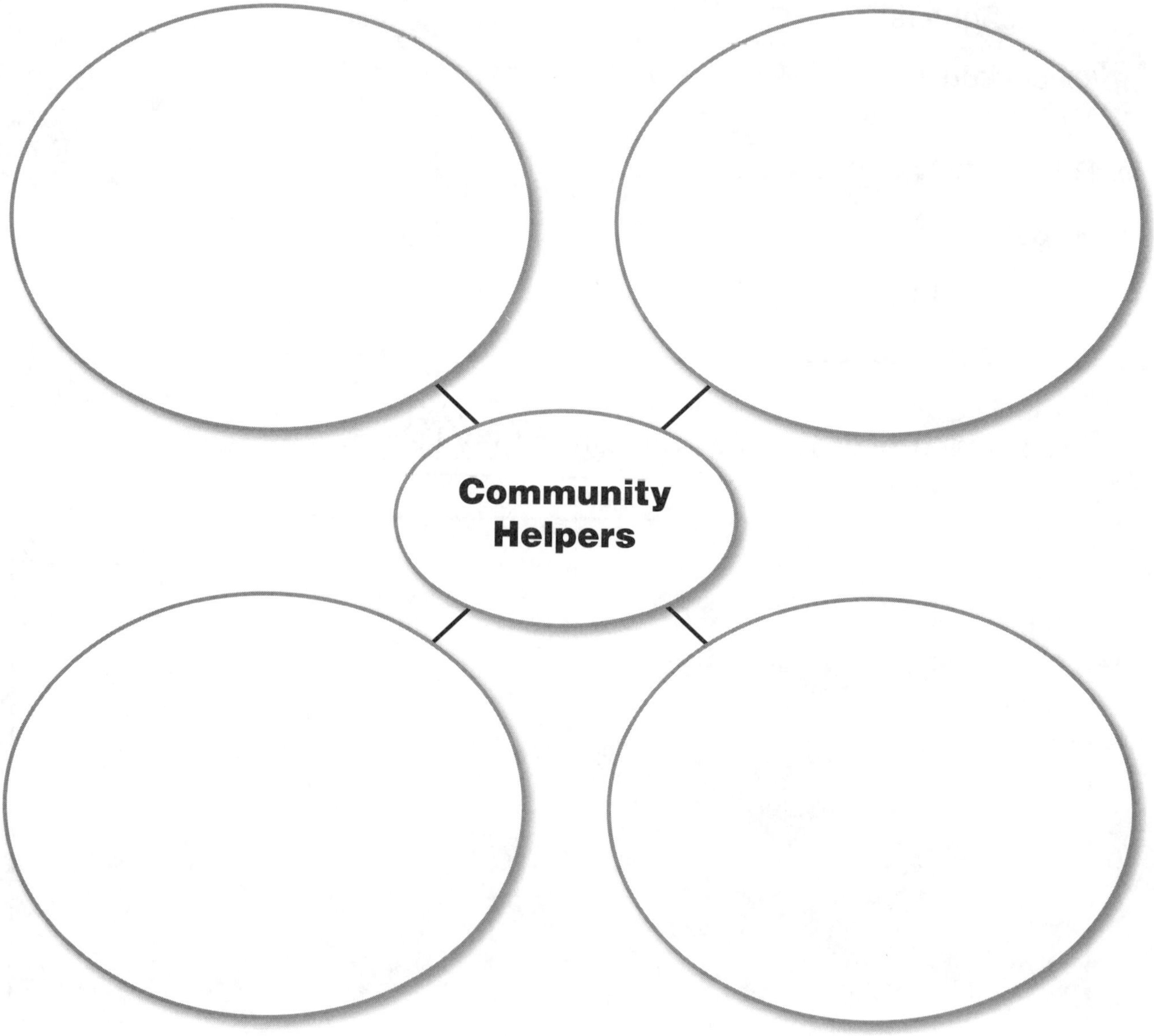

Name ___________________________________

UNIT 5

Community Helpers

Explain

Write a paragraph that explains **the important jobs that community helpers do.**

- Use information from your graphic organizer and the social studies article.

____

Title

____

____

____

____

____

____

____

____

____

____

One Milk, Please

Lesson Objectives

Writing
Students use information from the health article to write an explanatory paragraph.

Vocabulary
Students learn content vocabulary words and use those words to write about how milk helps humans.

Content Knowledge
Students understand that milk contains essential vitamins, such as calcium and iron.

Essential Understanding
Students understand that milk and other dairy products are an important part of the human diet.

Prepare

Reproduce and distribute one copy for each student.

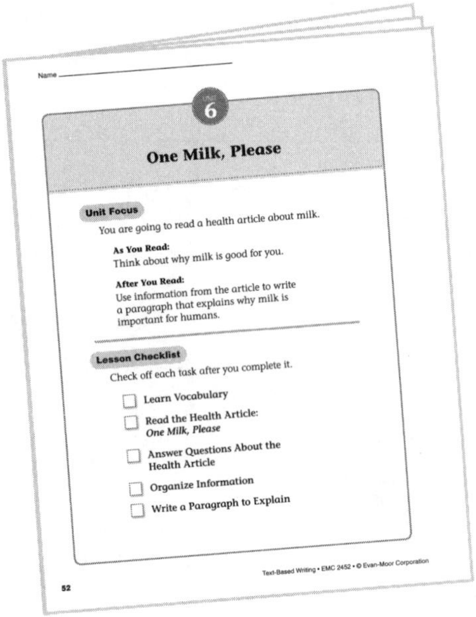
Name

6

One Milk, Please

Unit Focus
You are going to read a health article about milk.

As You Read:
Think about why milk is good for you.

After You Read:
Use information from the article to write a paragraph that explains why milk is important for humans.

Lesson Checklist
Check off each task after you complete it.

- ☐ Learn Vocabulary
- ☐ Read the Health Article: *One Milk, Please*
- ☐ Answer Questions About the Health Article
- ☐ Organize Information
- ☐ Write a Paragraph to Explain

52 Text-Based Writing • EMC 2452 • © Evan-Moor Corporation

1 Unit Focus and Lesson Checklist

Distribute one unit to each student and direct students' attention to the Unit Focus and Lesson Checklist. Tell them they will be able to refer to the focus of the unit as needed while working on the lessons. Instruct students to check off each task on the checklist after they complete it.

Read aloud the focus statements, and verify that students understand their purpose for reading. Ask:

- *What are we going to read about?* (milk)
- *What are you going to learn about milk?* (why it is good for you)
- *What are you going to write based on this article?* (a paragraph that explains)

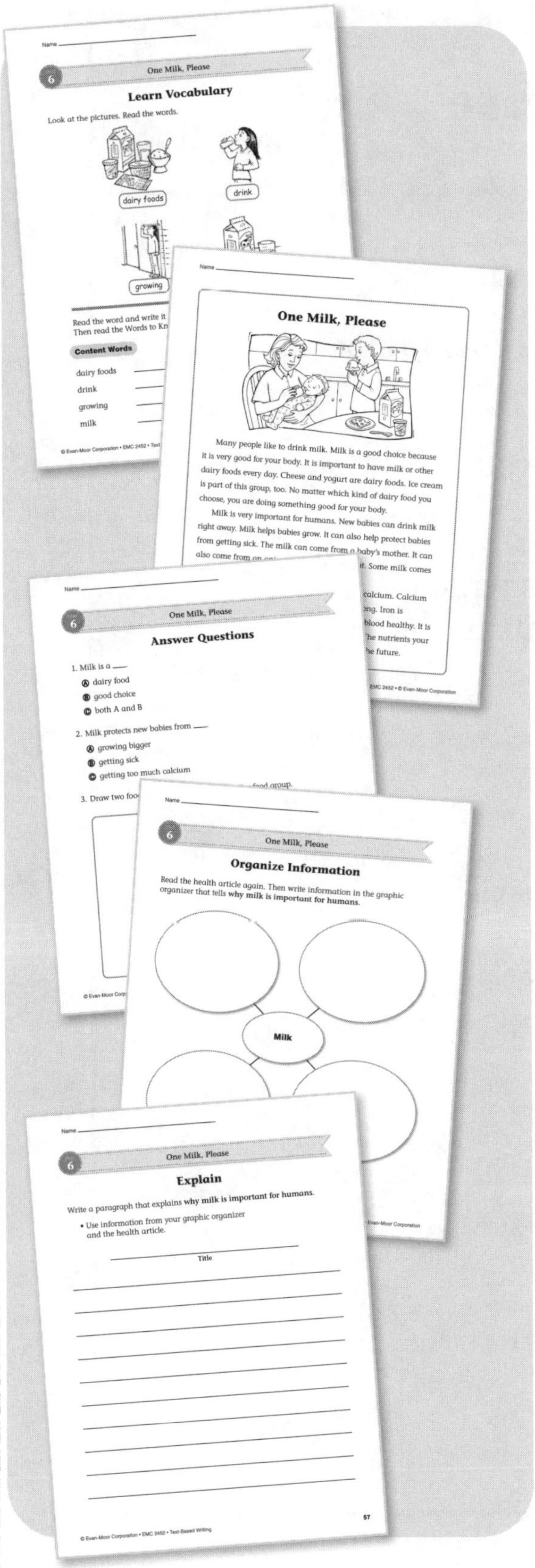

2 Learn Vocabulary

Direct students' attention to the picture dictionary. Read aloud each content vocabulary word and have students repeat. Point out that the words are related to milk and that students will have a better understanding of the words after they read the health article. Have students write the vocabulary words on the provided lines. Then review the Words to Know, and encourage students to ask questions about any words they do not understand.

3 Read the Health Article: *One Milk, Please*

Read aloud the health article as students follow along silently. Then have students reread the article independently or in small groups.

4 Answer Questions About the Health Article

To ensure reading comprehension, have students answer the text-dependent questions. Review the answers together.

5 Organize Information

Explain to students that they will use an idea-web graphic organizer to help them plan their paragraphs. Guide students in using the text to complete the organizer, rereading the article if needed.

Remind students that a paragraph that explains:

- tells why something is important, or
- tells why or how something works.

6 Write an Explanatory Paragraph

Instruct students to complete the writing assignment independently, with a partner, or in small groups.

If needed, review the structure of an explanatory paragraph:

- The topic sentence introduces the subject.
- Detail sentences explain the subject to the reader.

Name ______________________________

UNIT 6

One Milk, Please

Unit Focus

You are going to read a health article about milk.

As You Read:
Think about why milk is good for you.

After You Read:
Use information from the article to write a paragraph that explains why milk is important for humans.

Lesson Checklist

Check off each task after you complete it.

- ☐ **Learn Vocabulary**
- ☐ **Read the Health Article:** ***One Milk, Please***
- ☐ **Answer Questions About the Health Article**
- ☐ **Organize Information**
- ☐ **Write a Paragraph to Explain**

Name ______________________________

UNIT 6

One Milk, Please

Learn Vocabulary

Look at the pictures. Read the words.

dairy foods

drink

growing

milk

Read the word and write it on the line.
Then read the Words to Know.

Content Words

dairy foods ______________

drink ______________

growing ______________

milk ______________

Words to Know

calcium	iron
future	nutrients
healthy	protect
humans	vitamin

Name ______________________________

One Milk, Please

Many people like to drink milk. Milk is a good choice because it is very good for your body. It is important to have milk or other dairy foods every day. Cheese and yogurt are dairy foods. Ice cream is part of this group, too. No matter which kind of dairy food you choose, you are doing something good for your body.

Milk is very important for humans. New babies can drink milk right away. Milk helps babies grow. It can also help protect babies from getting sick. The milk can come from a baby's mother. It can also come from an animal, like a cow or a goat. Some milk comes from beans.

Milk has a lot of calcium. All humans need calcium. Calcium is a vitamin that keeps your teeth and bones strong. Iron is another vitamin that is in milk. Iron keeps your blood healthy. It is important to drink milk while you are growing. The nutrients your body gets from milk will help you stay strong in the future.

Name ______________________________

UNIT 6

One Milk, Please

Answer Questions

1. Milk is a ____.

   Ⓐ dairy food

   Ⓑ good choice

   Ⓒ both A and B

2. Milk protects new babies from ____.

   Ⓐ growing bigger

   Ⓑ getting sick

   Ⓒ getting too much calcium

3. Draw two foods you like to eat from the dairy food group.

Name ______________________________

UNIT 6 One Milk, Please

Organize Information

Read the health article again. Then write information in the graphic organizer that tells **why milk is important for humans**.

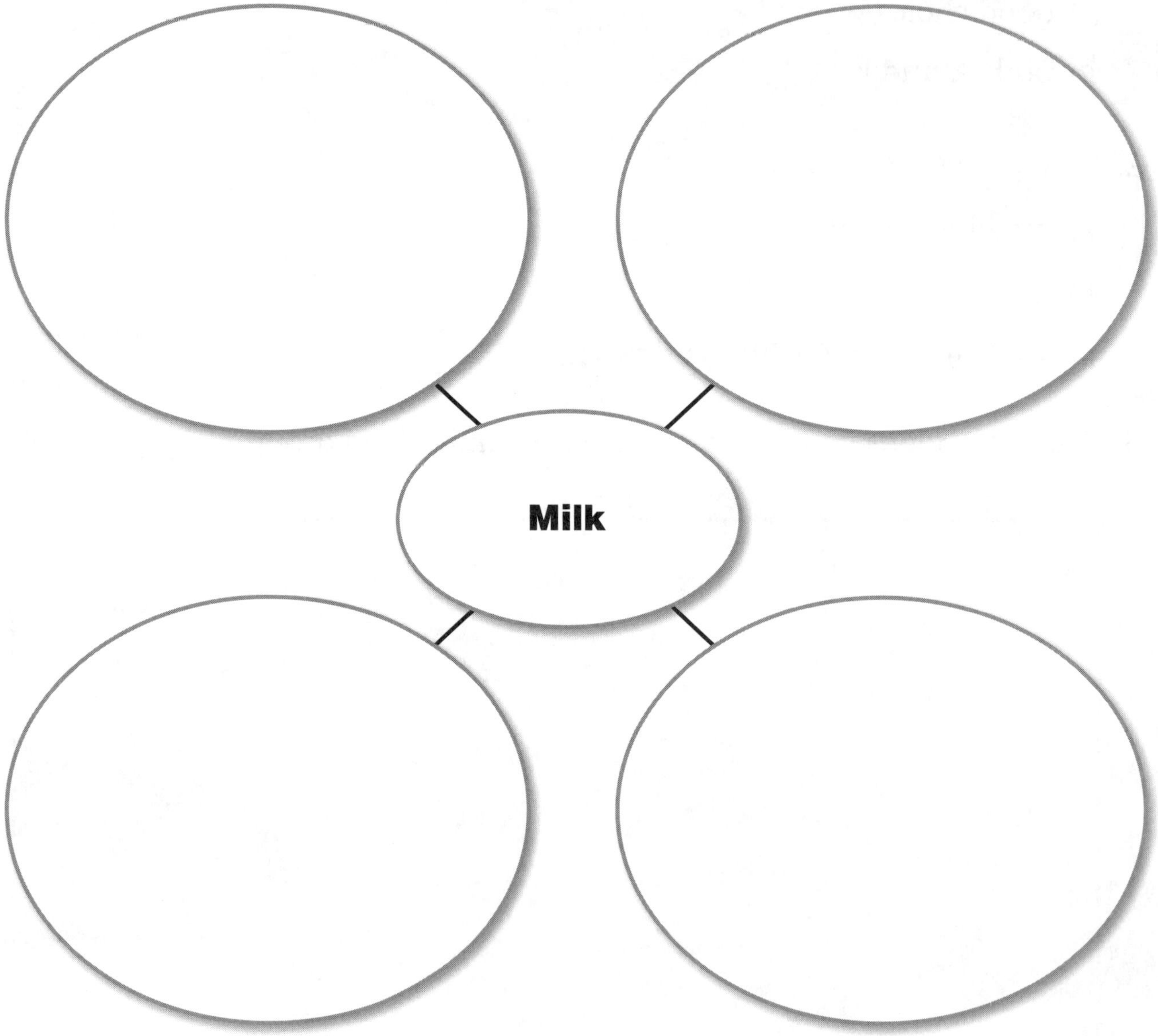

Name ___________________________________

UNIT 6

One Milk, Please

Explain

Write a paragraph that explains **why milk is important for humans.**

- Use information from your graphic organizer and the health article.

____
Title

The Great Lakes

Lesson Objectives

Writing
Students use information from the geography article to write an informative paragraph.

Vocabulary
Students learn content vocabulary words and use those words to write about the Great Lakes.

Content Knowledge
Students understand where the Great Lakes are located and what they look like.

Essential Understanding
Students understand how to find lakes on maps and use language to describe bodies of water.

Prepare

Reproduce and distribute one copy for each student.

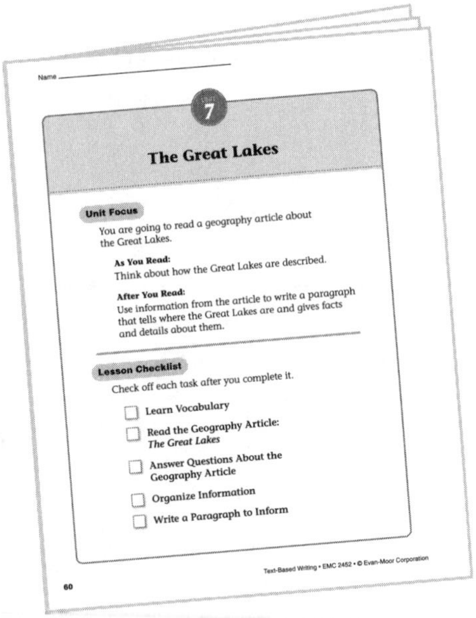
Name

UNIT 7

The Great Lakes

Unit Focus
You are going to read a geography article about the Great Lakes.

As You Read:
Think about how the Great Lakes are described.

After You Read:
Use information from the article to write a paragraph that tells where the Great Lakes are and gives facts and details about them.

Lesson Checklist
Check off each task after you complete it.

- ☐ Learn Vocabulary
- ☐ Read the Geography Article: *The Great Lakes*
- ☐ Answer Questions About the Geography Article
- ☐ Organize Information
- ☐ Write a Paragraph to Inform

60 Text-Based Writing • EMC 2452 • © Evan-Moor Corporation

1 Unit Focus and Lesson Checklist

Distribute one unit to each student and direct students' attention to the Unit Focus and Lesson Checklist. Tell them they will be able to refer to the focus of the unit as needed while working on the lessons. Instruct students to check off each task on the checklist after they complete it.

Read aloud the focus statements, and verify that students understand their purpose for reading. Ask:

- *What are we going to read about?* (the Great Lakes)
- *What are you going to learn about them?* (where they are; facts about them)
- *What are you going to write based on this article?* (a paragraph that informs)

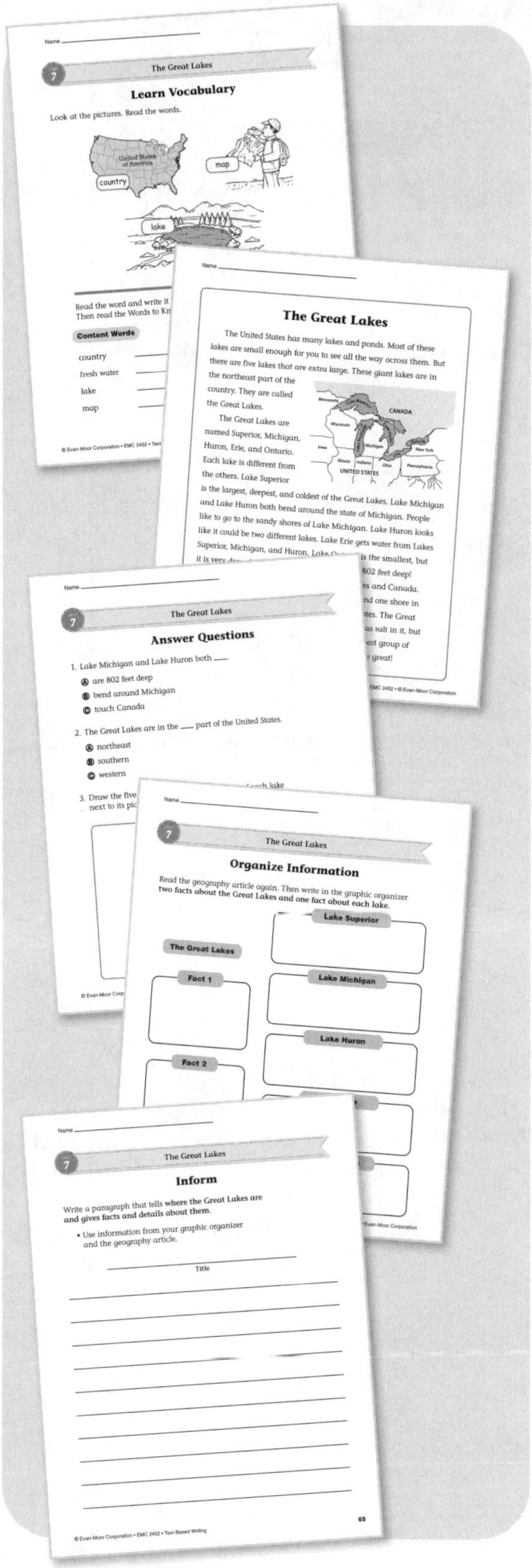

2 **Learn Vocabulary**

Direct students' attention to the picture dictionary. Read aloud each content vocabulary word and have students repeat. Point out that the words are related to the Great Lakes and that students will have a better understanding of the words after they read the geography article. Have students write the vocabulary words on the provided lines. Then review the Words to Know, and encourage students to ask questions about any words they do not understand.

3 **Read the Geography Article: *The Great Lakes***

Read aloud the geography article. Then have students reread the article independently or in small groups.

4 **Answer Questions About the Geography Article**

To ensure reading comprehension, have students answer the text-dependent questions. Review the answers together.

5 **Organize Information**

Explain to students that they will use an idea-web graphic organizer to help them plan their paragraphs. Guide students in using the text to complete the organizer, rereading the article if needed.

Remind students that a paragraph that informs:

- tells where something is, or
- tells facts and details about something.

6 **Write an Informative Paragraph**

Instruct students to complete the writing assignment independently, with a partner, or in small groups.

If needed, review the structure of an informative paragraph:

- The topic sentence introduces the subject.
- Detail sentences explain the subject to the reader.

Name ______________________________

UNIT 7

The Great Lakes

Unit Focus

You are going to read a geography article about the Great Lakes.

As You Read:
Think about how the Great Lakes are described.

After You Read:
Use information from the article to write a paragraph that tells where the Great Lakes are and gives facts and details about them.

Lesson Checklist

Check off each task after you complete it.

- ☐ **Learn Vocabulary**
- ☐ **Read the Geography Article:** ***The Great Lakes***
- ☐ **Answer Questions About the Geography Article**
- ☐ **Organize Information**
- ☐ **Write a Paragraph to Inform**

Name ______________________________

UNIT 7

The Great Lakes

Learn Vocabulary

Look at the pictures. Read the words.

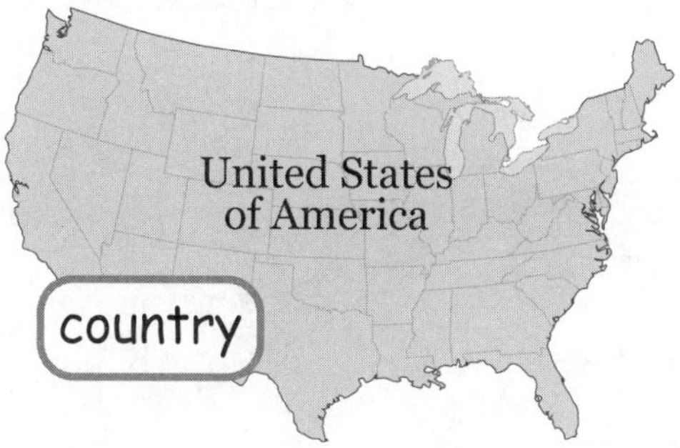

Read the word and write it on the line.
Then read the Words to Know.

Content Words

country ______________________

fresh water ______________________

lake ______________________

map ______________________

Words to Know

across	giant
bend	narrow
deepest	northeast
extra	shore

Name ________________________________

The Great Lakes

The United States has many lakes and ponds. Most of these lakes are small enough for you to see all the way across them. But there are five lakes that are extra large. These giant lakes are in the northeast part of the country. They are called the Great Lakes.

The Great Lakes are named Superior, Michigan, Huron, Erie, and Ontario. Each lake is different from the others. Lake Superior is the largest, deepest, and coldest of the Great Lakes. Lake Michigan and Lake Huron both bend around the state of Michigan. People like to go to the sandy shores of Lake Michigan. Lake Huron looks like it could be two different lakes. Lake Erie gets water from Lakes Superior, Michigan, and Huron. Lake Ontario is the smallest, but it is very deep. Some parts of Lake Ontario are 802 feet deep!

Four of the lakes are in both the United States and Canada. They each have one shore in the United States and one shore in Canada. Lake Michigan is only in the United States. The Great Lakes are made up of fresh water. Ocean water has salt in it, but fresh water does not. The Great Lakes are the largest group of lakes with fresh water in the world. They really are great!

Name ______________________________

UNIT 7 The Great Lakes

Answer Questions

1. Lake Michigan and Lake Huron both ____.

   Ⓐ are 802 feet deep

   Ⓑ bend around Michigan

   Ⓒ touch Canada

2. The Great Lakes are in the ____ part of the United States.

   Ⓐ northeast

   Ⓑ southern

   Ⓒ western

3. Draw the five Great Lakes. Write the name of each lake next to its picture.

Name ________________________________

UNIT 7 The Great Lakes

Organize Information

Read the geography article again. Then write in the graphic organizer **two facts about the Great Lakes and one fact about each lake.**

The Great Lakes

Fact 1

Fact 2

Lake Superior

Lake Michigan

Lake Huron

Lake Erie

Lake Ontario

Name ______________________________

UNIT 7

The Great Lakes

Inform

Write a paragraph that tells **where the Great Lakes are and gives facts and details about them.**

- Use information from your graphic organizer and the geography article.

____

Title

UNIT **8** Health Article – Level I

Cause-and-Effect Writing Prompt

Another Cold!

Lesson Objectives

Writing
Students use information from the health article to write a cause-and-effect paragraph.

Vocabulary
Students learn content vocabulary words and use those words to write about the common cold.

Content Knowledge
Students understand that colds are caused by germs and can be spread easily.

Essential Understanding
Students understand why people catch colds and how they can stay healthy.

Prepare

Reproduce and distribute one copy for each student.

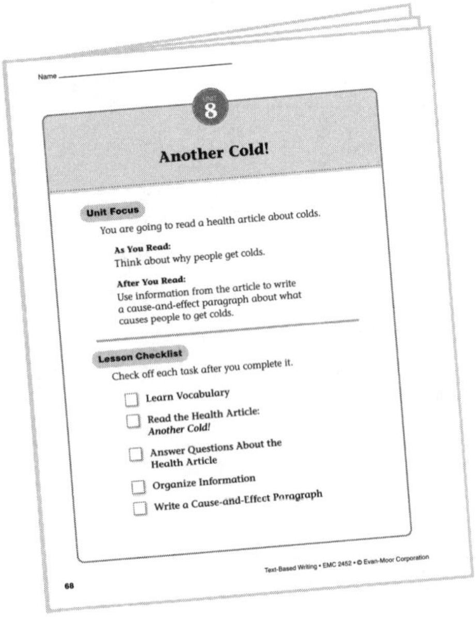
Name

UNIT 8

Another Cold!

Unit Focus

You are going to read a health article about colds.

As You Read:
Think about why people get colds.

After You Read:
Use information from the article to write a cause-and-effect paragraph about what causes people to get colds.

Lesson Checklist

Check off each task after you complete it.

- ☐ Learn Vocabulary
- ☐ Read the Health Article: *Another Cold!*
- ☐ Answer Questions About the Health Article
- ☐ Organize Information
- ☐ Write a Cause-and-Effect Paragraph

68 Text-Based Writing • EMC 2452 • © Evan-Moor Corporation

1 Unit Focus and Lesson Checklist

Distribute one unit to each student and direct students' attention to the Unit Focus and Lesson Checklist. Tell them they will be able to refer to the focus of the unit as needed while working on the lessons. Instruct students to check off each task on the checklist after they complete it.

Read aloud the focus statements, and verify that students understand their purpose for reading. Ask:

- *What are we going to read about?* (colds)
- *What are you going to learn about colds?* (what causes them)
- *What are you going to write based on this article?* (a cause-and-effect paragraph)

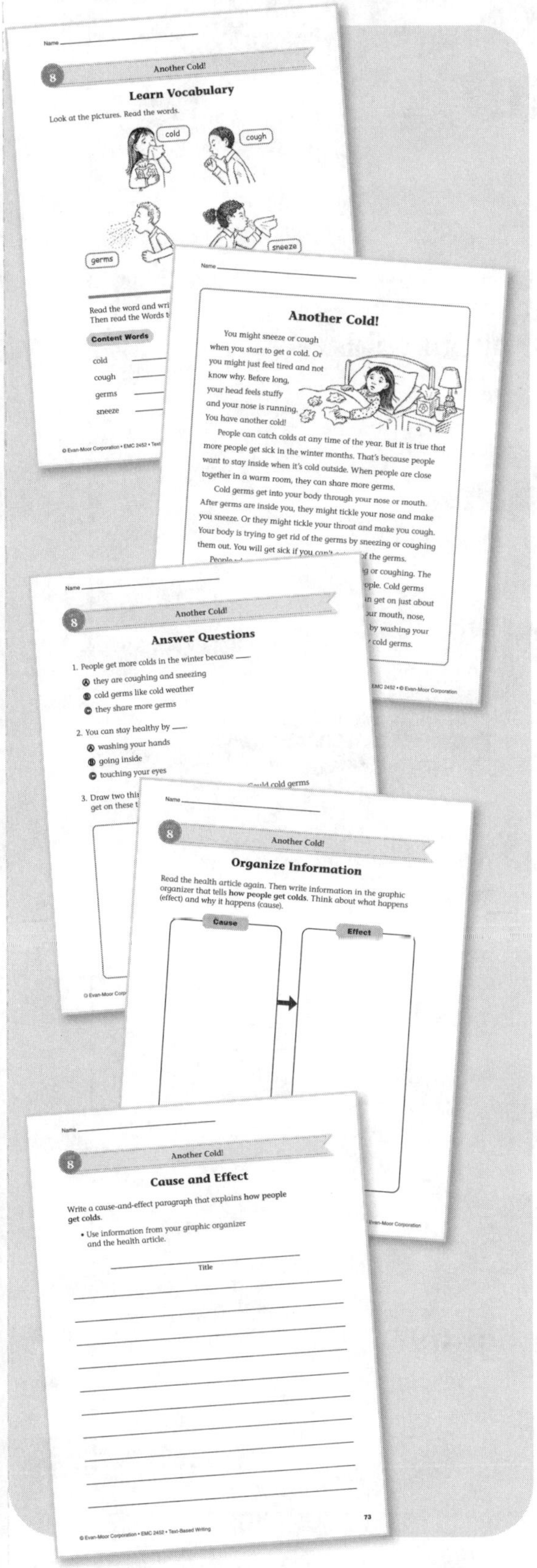

2 **Learn Vocabulary**
Direct students' attention to the picture dictionary. Read aloud each content vocabulary word and have students repeat. Point out that the words are related to colds and that students will have a better understanding of the words after they read the health article. Have students write the vocabulary words on the provided lines. Then review the Words to Know, and encourage students to ask questions about any words they do not understand.

3 **Read the Health Article: *Another Cold!***
Read aloud the health article as students follow along silently. Then have students reread the article independently or in small groups.

4 **Answer Questions About the Health Article**
To ensure reading comprehension, have students answer the text-dependent questions. Review the answers together.

5 **Organize Information**
Explain to students that they will use a cause-and-effect graphic organizer to help them plan their paragraphs. Guide students in using the text to complete the organizer, rereading the article if needed.

Remind students that a cause-and-effect paragraph:

- tells what happens (effect), and
- tells why it happens (cause).

6 **Write a Cause-and-Effect Paragraph**
Instruct students to complete the writing assignment independently, with a partner, or in small groups.

If needed, review the structure of a cause-and-effect paragraph:

- The topic sentence tells the cause-and-effect relationship.
- Details support the topic sentence and tell more about the cause and the effect.

Name ____________________

UNIT 8

Another Cold!

Unit Focus

You are going to read a health article about colds.

As You Read:
Think about why people get colds.

After You Read:
Use information from the article to write a cause-and-effect paragraph about what causes people to get colds.

Lesson Checklist

Check off each task after you complete it.

- ☐ **Learn Vocabulary**
- ☐ **Read the Health Article: *Another Cold!***
- ☐ **Answer Questions About the Health Article**
- ☐ **Organize Information**
- ☐ **Write a Cause-and-Effect Paragraph**

Name ______________________________

UNIT 8

Another Cold!

Learn Vocabulary

Look at the pictures. Read the words.

Read the word and write it on the line.
Then read the Words to Know.

Content Words

cold ______________________

cough ______________________

germs ______________________

sneeze ______________________

Words to Know

inside	tickle
outside	tired
share	touch
spread	winter

Name ____________________

Another Cold!

You might sneeze or cough when you start to get a cold. Or you might just feel tired and not know why. Before long, your head feels stuffy and your nose is running. You have another cold!

People can catch colds at any time of the year. But it is true that more people get sick in the winter months. That's because people want to stay inside when it's cold outside. When people are close together in a warm room, they can share more germs.

Cold germs get into your body through your nose or mouth. After germs are inside you, they might tickle your nose and make you sneeze. Or they might tickle your throat and make you cough. Your body is trying to get rid of the germs by sneezing or coughing them out. You will get sick if you can't get rid of the germs.

People who are sick spread colds by sneezing or coughing. The germs fly through the air and get onto other people. Cold germs can also end up on doorknobs or tables. They can get on just about anything. If you touch a germ and then touch your mouth, nose, or eyes, you can catch the cold. You can stay safe by washing your hands often. Warm water and soap will kill many cold germs.

Name ____________________

UNIT 8

Another Cold!

Answer Questions

1. People get more colds in the winter because ___.

   Ⓐ they are coughing and sneezing

   Ⓑ cold germs like cold weather

   Ⓒ they share more germs

2. You can stay healthy by ___.

   Ⓐ washing your hands

   Ⓑ going inside

   Ⓒ touching your eyes

3. Draw two things you use in your classroom. Could cold germs get on these things? Write *yes* or *no* beside each picture.

Name ________________________________

UNIT 8 Another Cold!

Organize Information

Read the health article again. Then write information in the graphic organizer that tells **how people get colds**. Think about what happens (effect) and why it happens (cause).

Cause		Effect
	→	
	→	

Name ____________________

UNIT 8 Another Cold!

Cause and Effect

Write a cause-and-effect paragraph that explains **how people get colds.**

- Use information from your graphic organizer and the health article.

____
Title

Earthworms in the Garden

Lesson Objectives

Writing
Students use information from the science article to write a cause-and-effect paragraph.

Vocabulary
Students learn content vocabulary words and use those words to write about how earthworms help plants grow.

Content Knowledge
Students understand that earthworms' living and eating habits help plants grow.

Essential Understanding
Students understand that plants and animals, including humans, depend upon each other to live and grow.

Prepare

Reproduce and distribute one copy for each student.

LESSON		PAGE
1	Unit Focus and Lesson Checklist	76
2	Learn Vocabulary	77
3	Read the Science Article: *Earthworms in the Garden*	78
4	Answer Questions About the Science Article	79
5	Organize Information	80
6	Write a Cause-and-Effect Paragraph	81

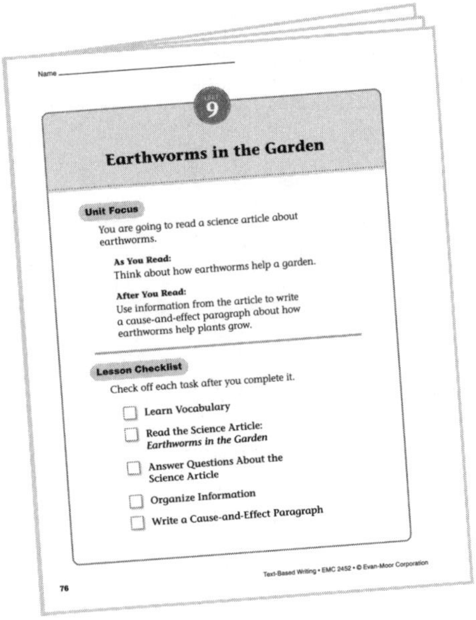
Name ____

9

Earthworms in the Garden

Unit Focus

You are going to read a science article about earthworms.

As You Read:
Think about how earthworms help a garden.

After You Read:
Use information from the article to write a cause-and-effect paragraph about how earthworms help plants grow.

Lesson Checklist

Check off each task after you complete it.

- ☐ Learn Vocabulary
- ☐ Read the Science Article: *Earthworms in the Garden*
- ☐ Answer Questions About the Science Article
- ☐ Organize Information
- ☐ Write a Cause-and-Effect Paragraph

76 Text-Based Writing • EMC 2452 • © Evan-Moor Corporation

1 Unit Focus and Lesson Checklist

Distribute one unit to each student and direct students' attention to the Unit Focus and Lesson Checklist. Tell them they will be able to refer to the focus of the unit as needed while working on the lessons. Instruct students to check off each task on the checklist after they complete it.

Read aloud the focus statements, and verify that students understand their purpose for reading. Ask:

- *What are we going to read about?* (earthworms)
- *What are you going to learn about earthworms?* (how they help a garden grow)
- *What are you going to write based on this article?* (a cause-and-effect paragraph)

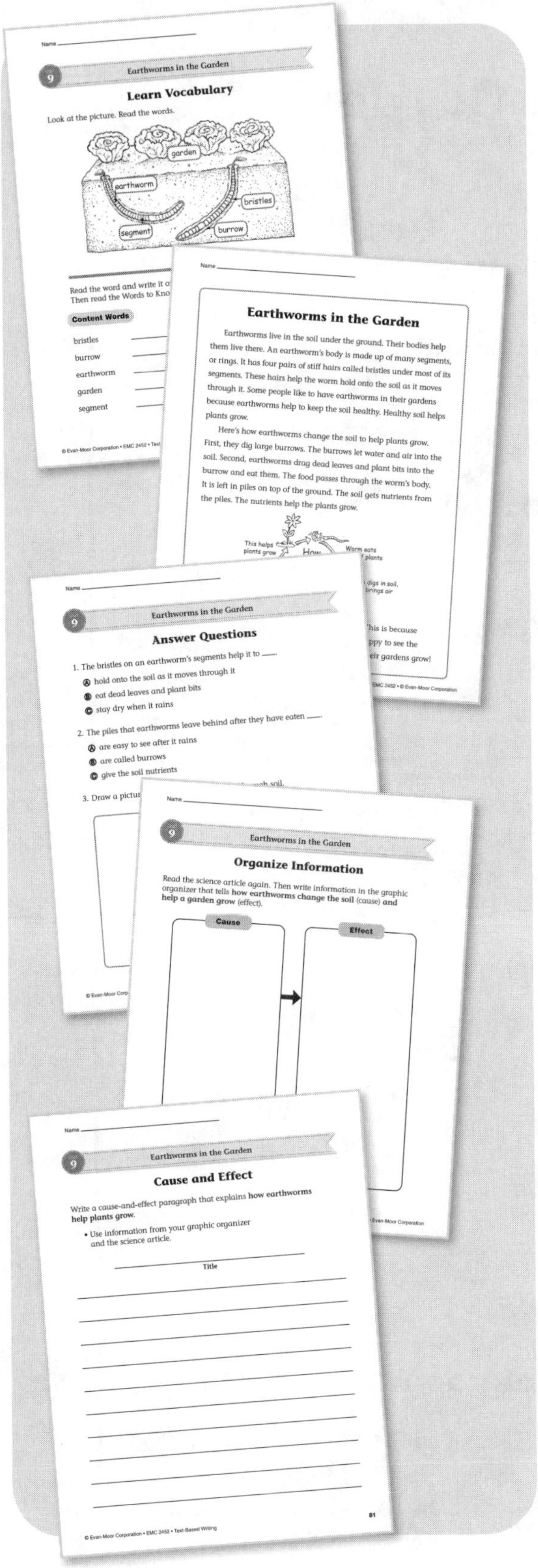

2 Learn Vocabulary

Direct students' attention to the picture dictionary. Read aloud each content vocabulary word and have students repeat. Point out that the words are related to earthworms and that students will have a better understanding of the words after they read the science article. Have students write the vocabulary words on the provided lines. Then review the Words to Know, and encourage students to ask questions about any words they do not understand.

3 Read the Science Article: *Earthworms in the Garden*

Read aloud the science article. Then have students reread the article independently or in small groups.

4 Answer Questions About the Science Article

To ensure reading comprehension, have students answer the text-dependent questions. Review the answers together.

5 Organize Information

Explain to students that they will use a cause-and-effect graphic organizer to help them plan their paragraphs. Guide students in using the text to complete the organizer, rereading the article if needed.

Remind students that a cause-and-effect paragraph:

- tells what happens (effect), and
- tells why it happens (cause).

6 Write a Cause-and-Effect Paragraph

Instruct students to complete the writing assignment independently, with a partner, or in small groups.

If needed, review the structure of a cause-and-effect paragraph:

- The topic sentence tells the cause-and-effect relationship.
- Details support the topic sentence and tell more about the cause and the effect.

Name ____________________

UNIT 9

Earthworms in the Garden

Unit Focus

You are going to read a science article about earthworms.

As You Read:

Think about how earthworms help a garden.

After You Read:

Use information from the article to write a cause-and-effect paragraph about how earthworms help plants grow.

Lesson Checklist

Check off each task after you complete it.

- ☐ **Learn Vocabulary**
- ☐ **Read the Science Article: *Earthworms in the Garden***
- ☐ **Answer Questions About the Science Article**
- ☐ **Organize Information**
- ☐ **Write a Cause-and-Effect Paragraph**

Name ___________________________________

UNIT 9

Earthworms in the Garden

Learn Vocabulary

Look at the picture. Read the words.

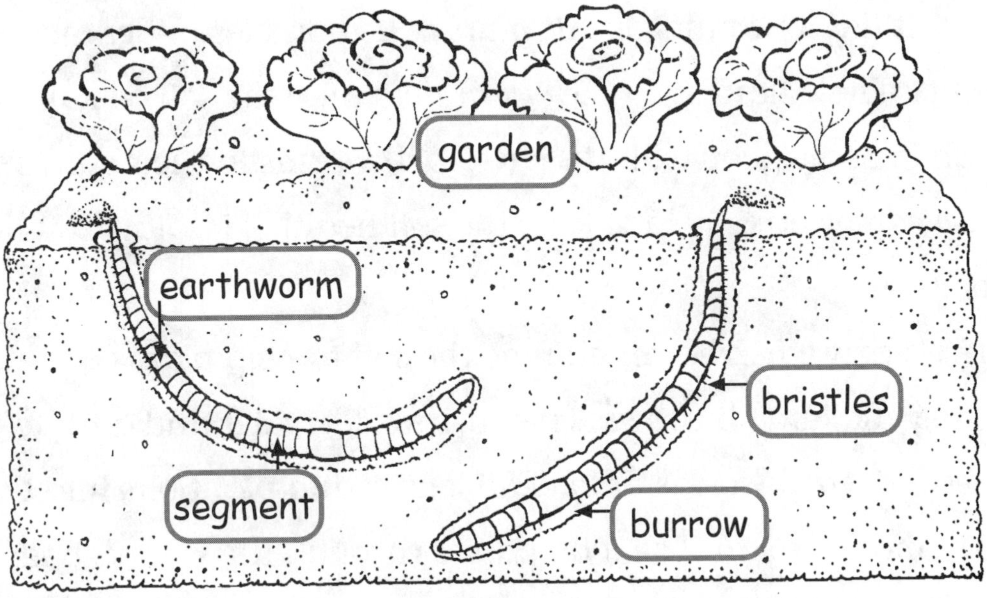

Read the word and write it on the line.
Then read the Words to Know.

Content Words

bristles ____________________

burrow ____________________

earthworm ____________________

garden ____________________

segment ____________________

Words to Know

bodies
soil
healthy
stiff
nutrients

Name ________________________________

Earthworms in the Garden

Earthworms live in the soil under the ground. Their bodies help them live there. An earthworm's body is made up of many segments, or rings. It has four pairs of stiff hairs called bristles under most of its segments. These hairs help the worm hold onto the soil as it moves through it. Some people like to have earthworms in their gardens because earthworms help to keep the soil healthy. Healthy soil helps plants grow.

Here's how earthworms change the soil to help plants grow. First, they dig large burrows. The burrows let water and air into the soil. Second, earthworms drag dead leaves and plant bits into the burrow and eat them. The food passes through the worm's body. It is left in piles on top of the ground. The soil gets nutrients from the piles. The nutrients help the plants grow.

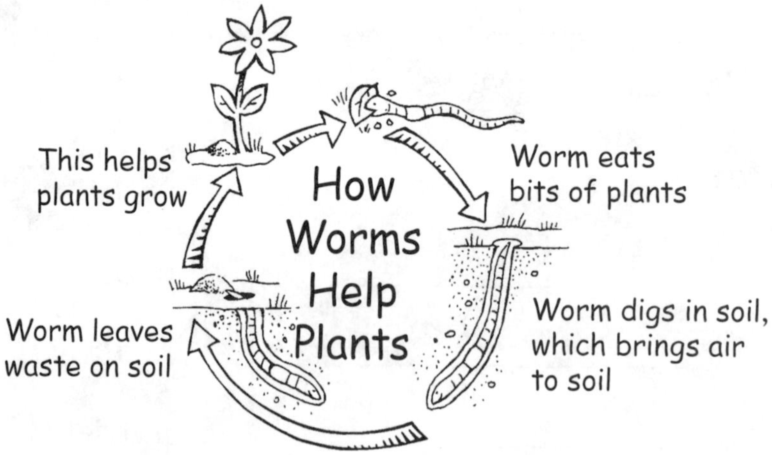

You can often see earthworms after it rains. This is because their burrows fill up with water. Gardeners are happy to see the earthworms. They know the worms are helping their gardens grow!

Name ____________________

UNIT 9

Earthworms in the Garden

Answer Questions

1. The bristles on an earthworm's segments help it to ___.

   Ⓐ hold onto the soil as it moves through it

   Ⓑ eat dead leaves and plant bits

   Ⓒ stay dry when it rains

2. The piles that earthworms leave behind after they have eaten ___.

   Ⓐ are easy to see after it rains

   Ⓑ are called burrows

   Ⓒ give the soil nutrients

3. Draw a picture of an earthworm moving through soil.

Name ______________________________

UNIT 9 — Earthworms in the Garden

Organize Information

Read the science article again. Then write information in the graphic organizer that tells **how earthworms change the soil** (cause) **and help a garden grow** (effect).

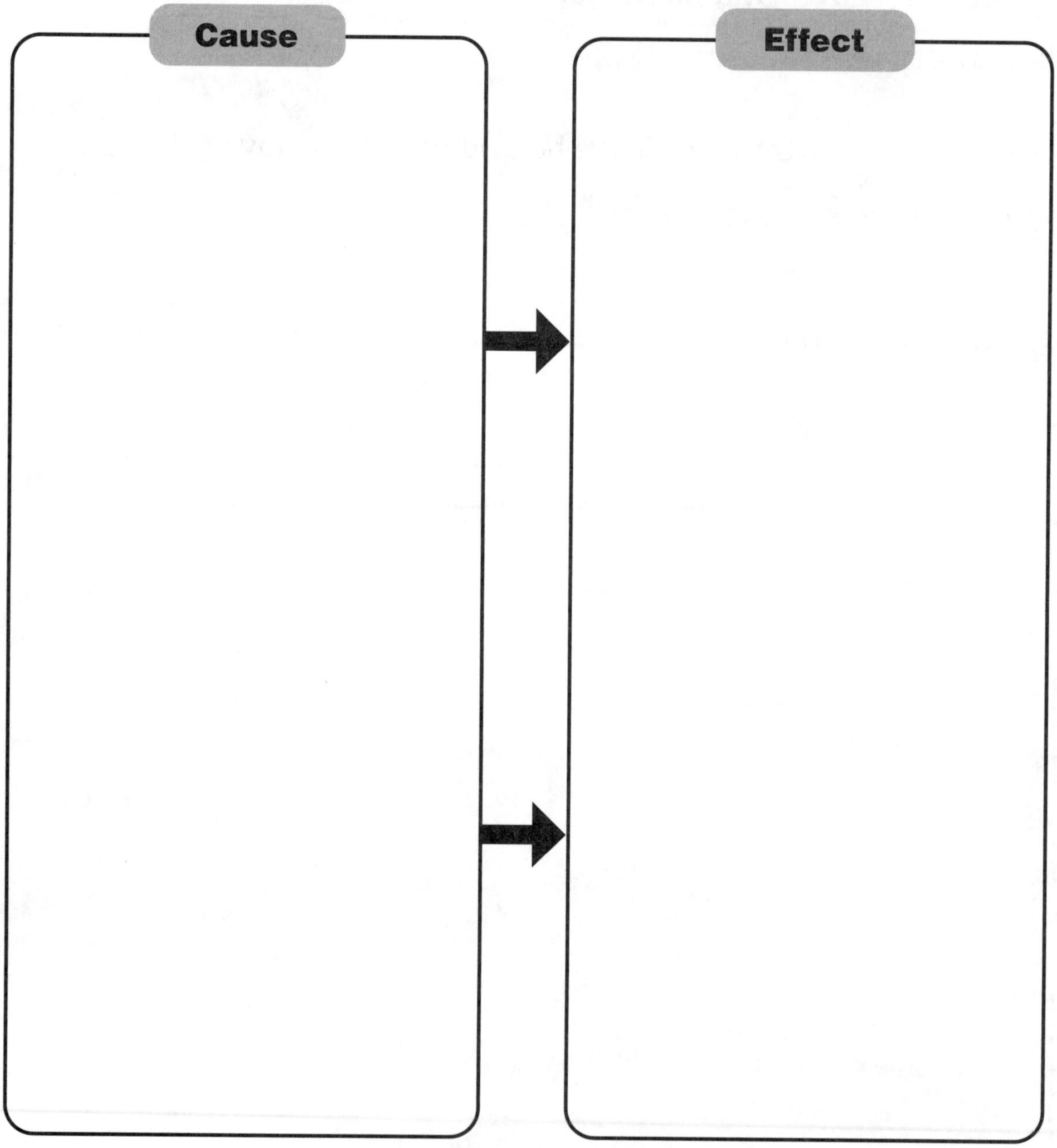

Name ______________________

UNIT 9 Earthworms in the Garden

Cause and Effect

Write a cause-and-effect paragraph that explains **how earthworms help plants grow.**

- Use information from your graphic organizer and the science article.

____

Title

Let's Work Together!

Lesson Objectives

Writing
Students use information from the social studies article to write an opinion paragraph.

Vocabulary
Students learn content vocabulary words and use those words to write about how playing on a sports team is beneficial.

Content Knowledge
Students understand that two or more people can work together to make a team.

Essential Understanding
Students understand that playing team sports now will help them work in teams in the future.

Prepare

Reproduce and distribute one copy for each student.

LESSON		PAGE
1	Unit Focus and Lesson Checklist	84
2	Learn Vocabulary	85
3	Read the Social Studies Article: *Let's Work Together!*	86
4	Answer Questions About the Social Studies Article	87
5	Organize Information	88
6	Write an Opinion Paragraph	89

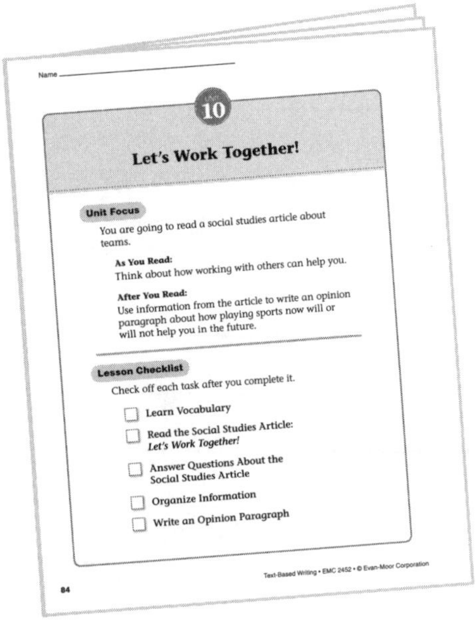
Name

10

Let's Work Together!

Unit Focus

You are going to read a social studies article about teams.

As You Read:
Think about how working with others can help you.

After You Read:
Use information from the article to write an opinion paragraph about how playing sports now will or will not help you in the future.

Lesson Checklist

Check off each task after you complete it.

- ☐ Learn Vocabulary
- ☐ Read the Social Studies Article: *Let's Work Together!*
- ☐ Answer Questions About the Social Studies Article
- ☐ Organize Information
- ☐ Write an Opinion Paragraph

84 Text-Based Writing • EMC 2452 • © Evan-Moor Corporation

1 Unit Focus and Lesson Checklist

Distribute one unit to each student and direct students' attention to the Unit Focus and Lesson Checklist. Tell them they will be able to refer to the focus of the unit as needed while working on the lessons. Instruct students to check off each task on the checklist after they complete it.

Read aloud the focus statements, and verify that students understand their purpose for reading. Ask:

- *What are we going to read about?* (teams)
- *What are you going to learn about teams?* (how they can help us)
- *What are you going to write based on this article?* (an opinion paragraph)

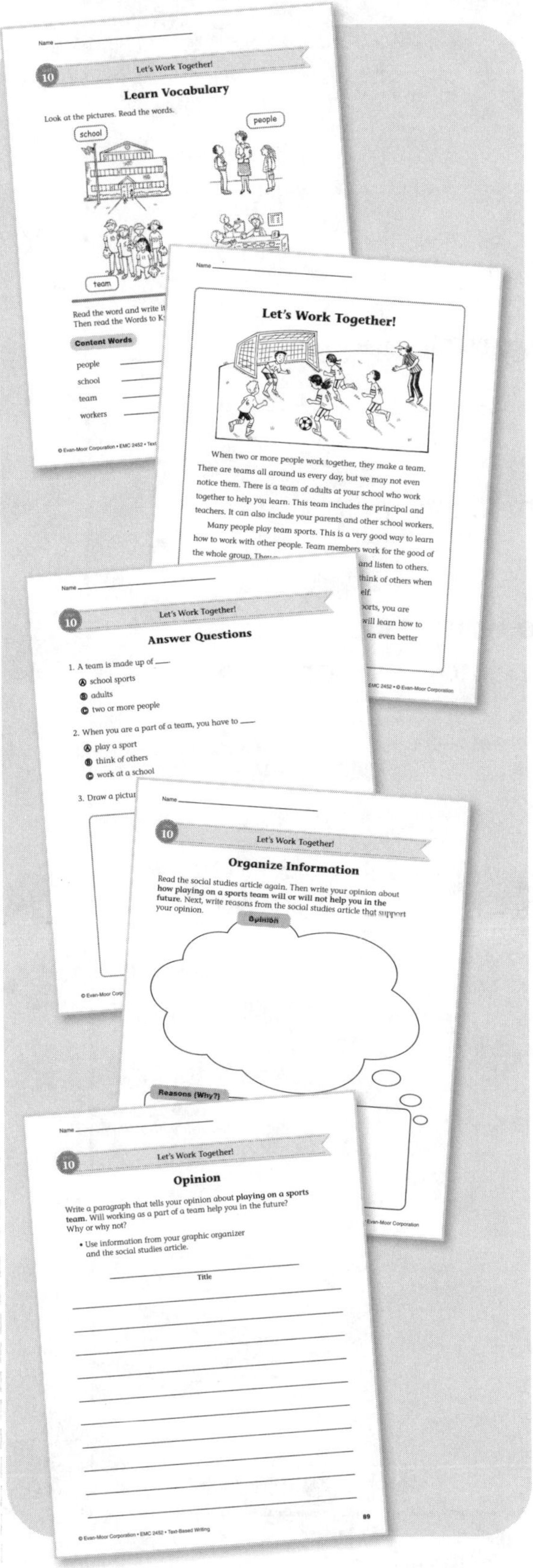

2 **Learn Vocabulary**

Direct students' attention to the picture dictionary. Read aloud each content vocabulary word and have students repeat. Point out that the words are related to teams and that students will have a better understanding of the words after they read the social studies article. Have students write the vocabulary words on the provided lines. Then review the Words to Know, and encourage students to ask questions about any words they do not understand.

3 **Read the Social Studies Article: *Let's Work Together!***

Read aloud the social studies article as students follow along silently. Then have students reread the article independently or in small groups.

4 **Answer Questions About the Social Studies Article**

To ensure reading comprehension, have students answer the text-dependent questions. Review the answers together.

5 **Organize Information**

Explain to students that they will use an opinion graphic organizer to help them plan their paragraphs. Guide students in using the text to complete the organizer, rereading the article if needed.

Remind students that an opinion paragraph:

- tells how you feel about something, and
- tells why you feel that way.

6 **Write an Opinion Paragraph**

Instruct students to complete the writing assignment independently, with a partner, or in small groups.

If needed, review the structure of an opinion paragraph:

- The topic sentence tells your opinion about the subject.
- Details give reasons for why you feel that way.

Name ______________________________

UNIT 10

Let's Work Together!

Unit Focus

You are going to read a social studies article about teams.

As You Read:
Think about how working with others can help you.

After You Read:
Use information from the article to write an opinion paragraph about how playing sports now will or will not help you in the future.

Lesson Checklist

Check off each task after you complete it.

- ☐ **Learn Vocabulary**
- ☐ **Read the Social Studies Article: *Let's Work Together!***
- ☐ **Answer Questions About the Social Studies Article**
- ☐ **Organize Information**
- ☐ **Write an Opinion Paragraph**

Name ______________________________

UNIT 10

Let's Work Together!

Learn Vocabulary

Look at the pictures. Read the words.

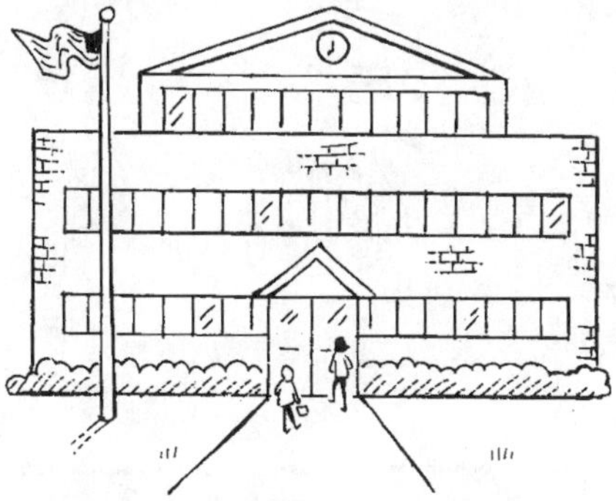

Read the word and write it on the line.
Then read the Words to Know.

Content Words

people ____________________

school ____________________

team ____________________

workers ____________________

Words to Know

adults	principal
group	skills
member	together
notice	work

Name ______________________________

Let's Work Together!

When two or more people work together, they make a team. There are teams all around us every day, but we may not even notice them. There is a team of adults at your school who work together to help you learn. This team includes the principal and teachers. It can also include your parents and other school workers.

Many people play team sports. This is a very good way to learn how to work with other people. Team members work for the good of the whole group. They practice, pay attention, and listen to others. They work together to win games. You have to think of others when you are on a team. You can't think of just yourself.

When you work with others at school or in sports, you are practicing skills you will need in the future. You will learn how to be a good team member now. This will make you an even better team member when you grow up!

Name ___________________________________

Answer Questions

1. A team is made up of ____.

   Ⓐ school sports

   Ⓑ adults

   Ⓒ two or more people

2. When you are a part of a team, you have to ____.

   Ⓐ play a sport

   Ⓑ think of others

   Ⓒ work at a school

3. Draw a picture of your favorite sports team.

Name ________________________________

UNIT 10 Let's Work Together!

Organize Information

Read the social studies article again. Then write your opinion about **how playing on a sports team will or will not help you in the future**. Next, write reasons from the social studies article that support your opinion.

Opinion

Reasons (Why?)

Name ____________________

UNIT 10

Let's Work Together!

Opinion

Write a paragraph that tells your opinion about **playing on a sports team**. Will working as a part of a team help you in the future? Why or why not?

- Use information from your graphic organizer and the social studies article.

____

Title

UNIT 11

Social Studies Article – Level J

Opinion Writing Prompt

Too Much Garbage

Lesson Objectives

Writing

Students use information from the social studies article to write an opinion paragraph.

Vocabulary

Students learn content vocabulary words and use those words to write their opinions about recycling.

Content Knowledge

Students understand that recycling can help keep garbage out of landfills.

Essential Understanding

Students understand that people can reuse things to keep Earth and humans safe and healthy.

Prepare

Reproduce and distribute one copy for each student.

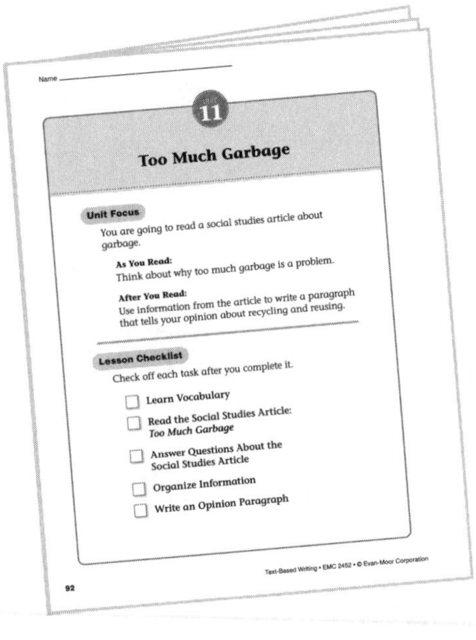
Name

11

Too Much Garbage

Unit Focus

You are going to read a social studies article about garbage.

As You Read:
Think about why too much garbage is a problem.

After You Read:
Use information from the article to write a paragraph that tells your opinion about recycling and reusing.

Lesson Checklist

Check off each task after you complete it.

- ☐ Learn Vocabulary
- ☐ Read the Social Studies Article: *Too Much Garbage*
- ☐ Answer Questions About the Social Studies Article
- ☐ Organize Information
- ☐ Write an Opinion Paragraph

92

Text-Based Writing • EMC 2452 • © Evan-Moor Corporation

1 Unit Focus and Lesson Checklist

Distribute one unit to each student and direct students' attention to the Unit Focus and Lesson Checklist. Tell them they will be able to refer to the focus of the unit as needed while working on the lessons. Instruct students to check off each task on the checklist after they complete it.

Read aloud the focus statements, and verify that students understand their purpose for reading. Ask:

- *What are we going to read about?* (garbage)
- *What are you going to learn about it?* (why it's a problem)
- *What are you going to write based on this article?* (an opinion paragraph)

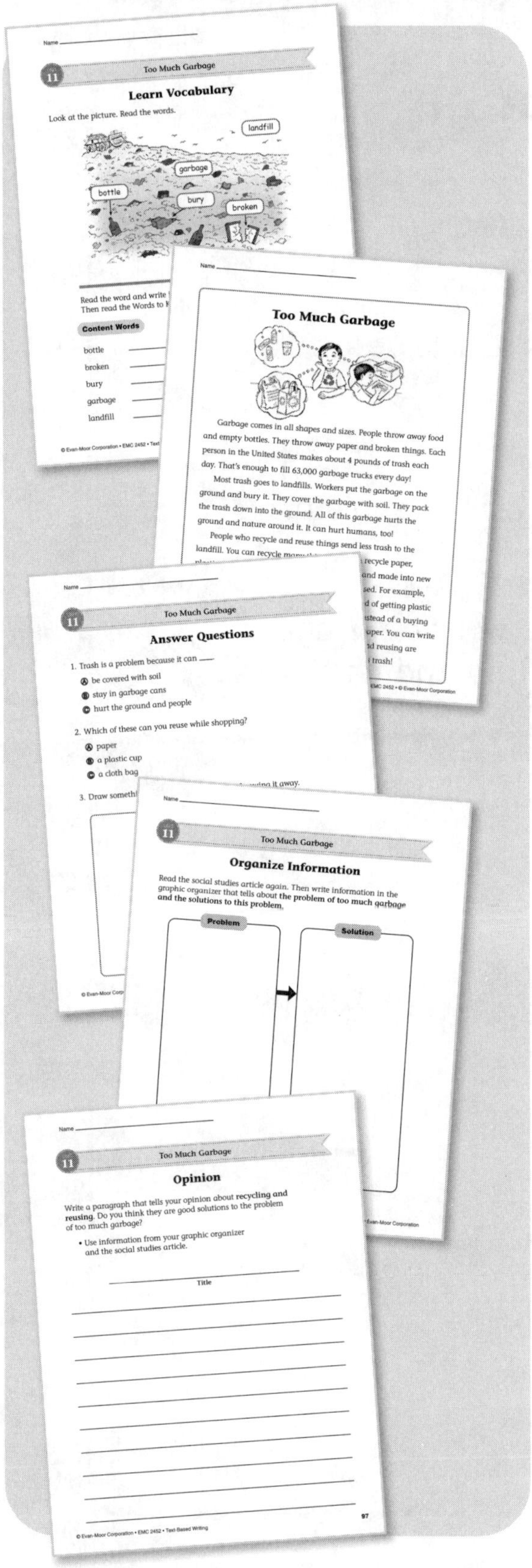

2 Learn Vocabulary

Direct students' attention to the picture dictionary. Read aloud each content vocabulary word and have students repeat. Point out that the words are related to garbage and that students will have a better understanding of the words after they read the social studies article. Have students write the vocabulary words on the provided lines. Then review the Words to Know, and encourage students to ask questions about any words they do not understand.

3 Read the Social Studies Article: *Too Much Garbage*

Read aloud the social studies article as students follow along silently. Then have students reread the article independently or in small groups.

4 Answer Questions About the Social Studies Article

To ensure reading comprehension, have students answer the text-dependent questions. Review the answers together.

5 Organize Information

Explain to students that they will use an opinion graphic organizer to help them plan their paragraphs. Guide students in using the text to complete the organizer, rereading the article if needed.

Remind students that an opinion paragraph:

- tells how you feel about something, and
- tells why you feel that way.

6 Write an Opinion Paragraph

Instruct students to complete the writing assignment independently, with a partner, or in small groups.

If needed, review the structure of an opinion paragraph:

- The topic sentence tells how you feel about the subject.
- Details give reasons that support your opinion.

Name ____________________

UNIT 11

Too Much Garbage

Unit Focus

You are going to read a social studies article about garbage.

As You Read:
Think about why too much garbage is a problem.

After You Read:
Use information from the article to write a paragraph that tells your opinion about recycling and reusing.

Lesson Checklist

Check off each task after you complete it.

- [ ] **Learn Vocabulary**
- [ ] **Read the Social Studies Article:** ***Too Much Garbage***
- [ ] **Answer Questions About the Social Studies Article**
- [ ] **Organize Information**
- [ ] **Write an Opinion Paragraph**

Name ______________________________

UNIT 11

Too Much Garbage

Learn Vocabulary

Look at the picture. Read the words.

Read the word and write it on the line.
Then read the Words to Know.

Content Words

bottle ______________

broken ______________

bury ______________

garbage ______________

landfill ______________

Words to Know

cloth	recycle
empty	reuse
nature	soil
plastic	trash

Name ___________________________

Too Much Garbage

Garbage comes in all shapes and sizes. People throw away food and empty bottles. They throw away paper and broken things. Each person in the United States makes about 4 pounds of trash each day. That's enough to fill 63,000 garbage trucks every day!

Most trash goes to landfills. Workers put the garbage on the ground and bury it. They cover the garbage with soil. They pack the trash down into the ground. All of this garbage hurts the ground and nature around it. It can hurt humans, too!

People who recycle and reuse things send less trash to the landfill. You can recycle many things. You can recycle paper, plastic, and glass. They can be smashed down and made into new things. You can also buy things that can be reused. For example, you can buy a cloth bag to take shopping instead of getting plastic bags from the store. You can drink from a cup instead of a buying a drink in a can. You can also reuse things like paper. You can write on both sides instead of just one side. Recycling and reusing are easy to do. People who recycle and reuse make less trash!

Name ________________________________

UNIT 11

Too Much Garbage

Answer Questions

1. Trash is a problem because it can ____.

   Ⓐ be covered with soil

   Ⓑ stay in garbage cans

   Ⓒ hurt the ground and people

2. Which of these can you reuse while shopping?

   Ⓐ paper

   Ⓑ a plastic cup

   Ⓒ a cloth bag

3. Draw something you can reuse instead of throwing it away.

Name ______________________________

UNIT 11 Too Much Garbage

Organize Information

Read the social studies article again. Then write information in the graphic organizer that tells about **the problem of too much garbage and the solutions to this problem.**

Problem		Solution
	→	
	→	

Name ______________________________

UNIT 11 Too Much Garbage

Opinion

Write a paragraph that tells your opinion about **recycling and reusing**. Do you think they are good solutions to the problem of too much garbage?

- Use information from your graphic organizer and the social studies article.

____

Title

____

____

____

____

____

____

____

____

____

____

Washington's Barn

Lesson Objectives

Writing
Students use information from the social studies article to write an opinion paragraph.

Vocabulary
Students learn content vocabulary words and use those words to write about how George Washington solved a problem.

Content Knowledge
Students understand that Washington's barn made harvesting wheat easier.

Essential Understanding
Students understand that people can solve problems by trying new things.

Prepare

Reproduce and distribute one copy for each student.

	LESSON	PAGE
1	Unit Focus and Lesson Checklist	100
2	Learn Vocabulary	101
3	Read the Social Studies Article: *Washington's Barn*	102
4	Answer Questions About the Social Studies Article	103
5	Organize Information	104
6	Write an Opinion Paragraph	105

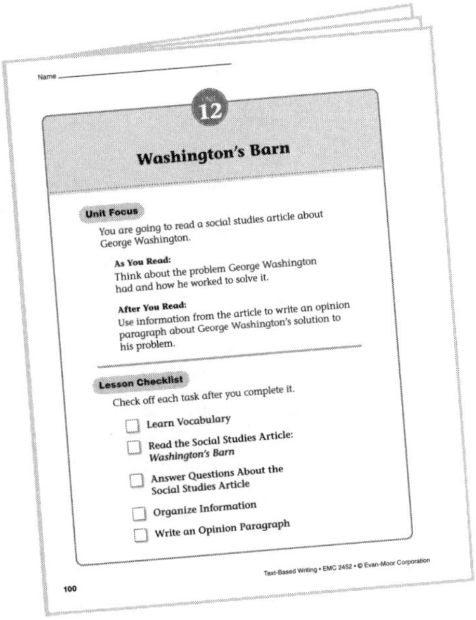

Name ____________

12

Washington's Barn

Unit Focus
You are going to read a social studies article about George Washington.

As You Read:
Think about the problem George Washington had and how he worked to solve it.

After You Read:
Use information from the article to write an opinion paragraph about George Washington's solution to his problem.

Lesson Checklist
Check off each task after you complete it.

- ☐ Learn Vocabulary
- ☐ Read the Social Studies Article: *Washington's Barn*
- ☐ Answer Questions About the Social Studies Article
- ☐ Organize Information
- ☐ Write an Opinion Paragraph

100 Text-Based Writing • EMC 2452 • © Evan-Moor Corporation

1 Unit Focus and Lesson Checklist

Distribute one unit to each student and direct students' attention to the Unit Focus and Lesson Checklist. Tell them they will be able to refer to the focus of the unit as needed while working on the lessons. Instruct students to check off each task on the checklist after they complete it.

Read aloud the focus statements, and verify that students understand their purpose for reading. Ask:

- *Who are we going to read about?* (George Washington)
- *What are you going to learn about him?* (how he solved a problem)
- *What are you going to write based on this article?* (an opinion paragraph)

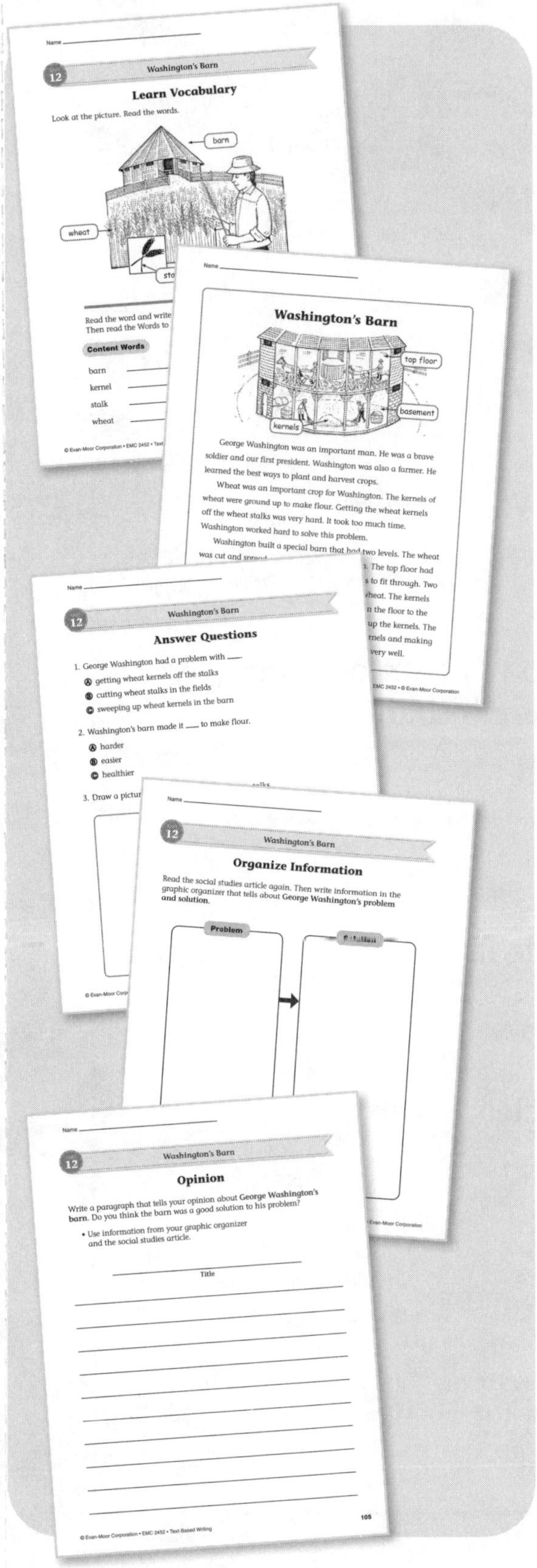

2 Learn Vocabulary

Direct students' attention to the picture dictionary. Read aloud each content vocabulary word and have students repeat. Point out that the words are related to farming and that students will have a better understanding of the words after they read the social studies article. Have students write the vocabulary words on the provided lines. Then review the Words to Know, and encourage students to ask questions about any words they do not understand.

3 Read the Social Studies Article: *Washington's Barn*

Read aloud the social studies article as students follow along silently. Then have students reread the article independently or in small groups.

4 Answer Questions About the Social Studies Article

To ensure reading comprehension, have students answer the text-dependent questions. Review the answers together.

5 Organize Information

Explain to students that they will use an opinion graphic organizer to help them plan their paragraphs. Guide students in using the text to complete the organizer, rereading the article if needed.

Remind students that an opinion paragraph:

- tells how you feel about something, and
- tells why you feel that way.

6 Write an Opinion Paragraph

Instruct students to complete the writing assignment independently, with a partner, or in small groups.

If needed, review the structure of an opinion paragraph:

- The topic sentence tells your opinion about the subject.
- Details give reasons why you feel that way.

Name ____

UNIT 12

Washington's Barn

Unit Focus

You are going to read a social studies article about George Washington.

As You Read:
Think about the problem George Washington had and how he worked to solve it.

After You Read:
Use information from the article to write an opinion paragraph about George Washington's solution to his problem.

Lesson Checklist

Check off each task after you complete it.

- ☐ **Learn Vocabulary**
- ☐ **Read the Social Studies Article: *Washington's Barn***
- ☐ **Answer Questions About the Social Studies Article**
- ☐ **Organize Information**
- ☐ **Write an Opinion Paragraph**

Name ____________________

UNIT 12

Washington's Barn

Learn Vocabulary

Look at the picture. Read the words.

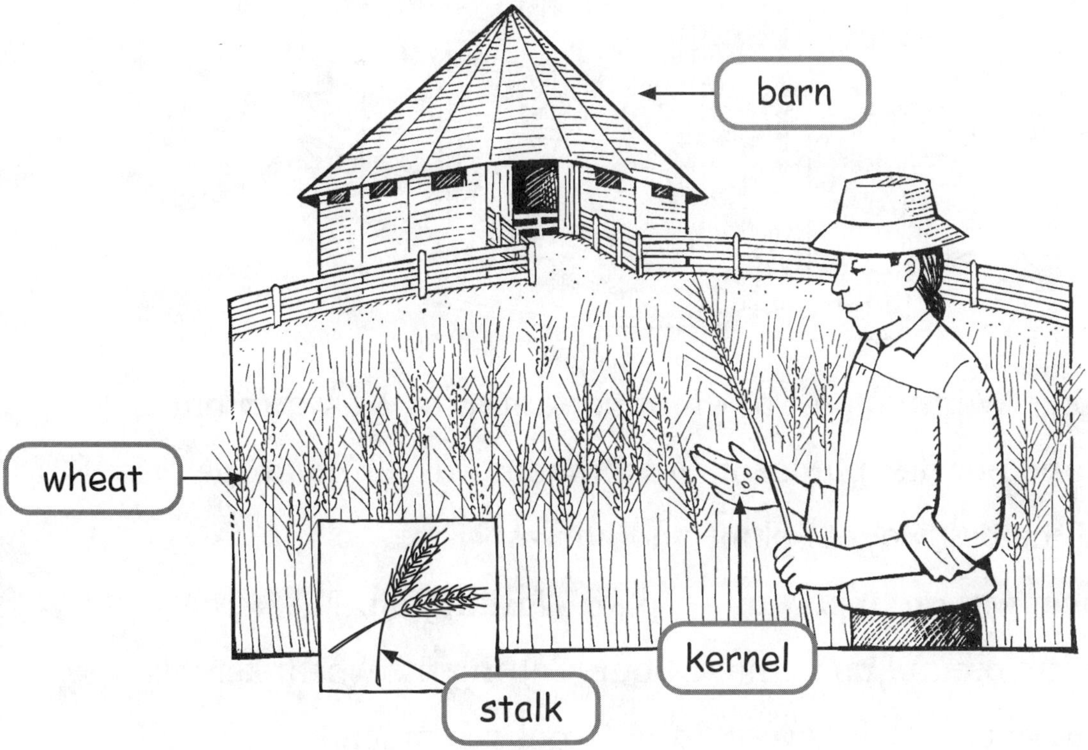

Read the word and write it on the line.
Then read the Words to Know.

Content Words

barn ____________________

kernel ____________________

stalk ____________________

wheat ____________________

Words to Know

basement	process
crops	solve
farmer	spread
harvest	swept

Name ________________________

Washington's Barn

George Washington was an important man. He was a brave soldier and our first president. Washington was also a farmer. He learned the best ways to plant and harvest crops.

Wheat was an important crop for Washington. The kernels of wheat were ground up to make flour. Getting the wheat kernels off the wheat stalks was very hard. It took too much time. Washington worked hard to solve this problem.

Washington built a special barn that had two levels. The wheat was cut and spread on the top floor of the barn. The top floor had small holes that were just big enough for kernels to fit through. Two horses came inside and walked around on the wheat. The kernels came off the stalks. They fell through the holes in the floor to the basement below. Workers in the basement swept up the kernels. The wheat barn made the process of getting wheat kernels and making flour easier and faster. Washington's plan worked very well.

Name ___________________________________

UNIT 12

Washington's Barn

Answer Questions

1. George Washington had a problem with ___.

   Ⓐ getting wheat kernels off the stalks

   Ⓑ cutting wheat stalks in the fields

   Ⓒ sweeping up wheat kernels in the barn

2. Washington's barn made it ___ to make flour.

   Ⓐ harder

   Ⓑ easier

   Ⓒ healthier

3. Draw a picture of a horse walking on wheat stalks.

Name ____

UNIT 12 Washington's Barn

Organize Information

Read the social studies article again. Then write information in the graphic organizer that tells about **George Washington's problem and solution**.

Problem	Solution

Name ______________________________

UNIT 12

Washington's Barn

Opinion

Write a paragraph that tells your opinion about **George Washington's barn**. Do you think the barn was a good solution to his problem?

- Use information from your graphic organizer and the social studies article.

____

Title

Thurgood Marshall

Lesson Objectives

Writing
Students use information from the biography to write an opinion paragraph.

Vocabulary
Students learn content vocabulary words and use those words to write about how Thurgood Marshall helped others.

Content Knowledge
Students understand that Thurgood Marshall helped to end segregation.

Essential Understanding
Students understand that it is important to treat others equally and help those in need.

Prepare

Reproduce and distribute one copy for each student.

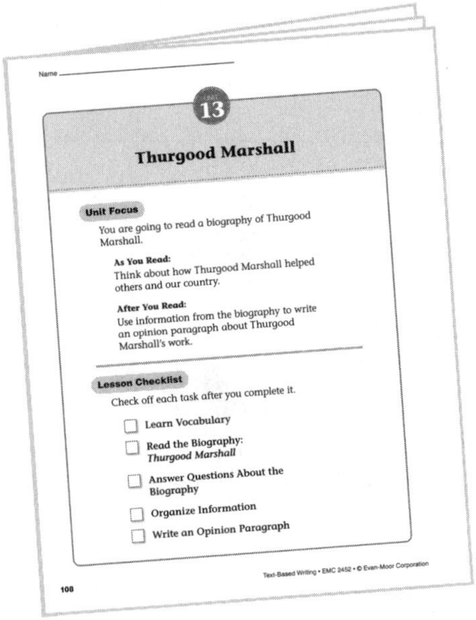
Name

13

Thurgood Marshall

Unit Focus
You are going to read a biography of Thurgood Marshall.
As You Read:
Think about how Thurgood Marshall helped others and our country.
After You Read:
Use information from the biography to write an opinion paragraph about Thurgood Marshall's work.

Lesson Checklist
Check off each task after you complete it.
- [ ] Learn Vocabulary
- [ ] Read the Biography: *Thurgood Marshall*
- [ ] Answer Questions About the Biography
- [ ] Organize Information
- [ ] Write an Opinion Paragraph

108 Text-Based Writing • EMC 2452 • © Evan-Moor Corporation

1 Unit Focus and Lesson Checklist

Distribute one unit to each student and direct students' attention to the Unit Focus and Lesson Checklist. Tell them they will be able to refer to the focus of the unit as needed while working on the lessons. Instruct students to check off each task on the checklist after they complete it.

Read aloud the focus statements, and verify that students understand their purpose for reading. Ask:

- *Who are we going to read about?* (Thurgood Marshall)
- *What are you going to learn about him?* (how he helped other people)
- *What are you going to write based on this biography?* (an opinion paragraph)

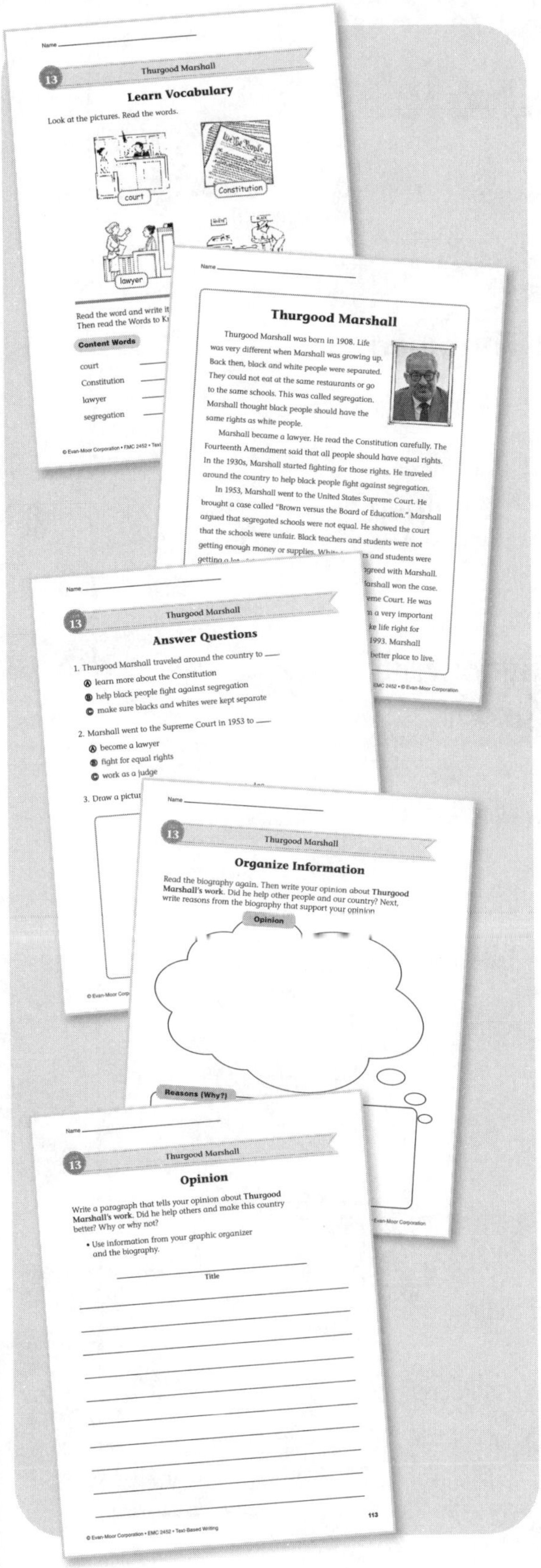

2 Learn Vocabulary

Direct students' attention to the picture dictionary. Read aloud each content vocabulary word and have students repeat. Point out that the words are related to Thurgood Marshall's work and that students will have a better understanding of the words after they read the biography. Have students write the vocabulary words on the provided lines. Then review the Words to Know, and encourage students to ask questions about any words they do not understand.

3 Read the Biography: *Thurgood Marshall*

Read aloud the biography as students follow along silently. Then have students reread the biography independently or in small groups.

4 Answer Questions About the Biography

To ensure reading comprehension, have students answer the text-dependent questions. Review the answers together.

5 Organize Information

Explain to students that they will use an opinion graphic organizer to help them plan their paragraphs. Guide students in using the text to complete the organizer, rereading the biography if needed.

Remind students that an opinion paragraph:

- tells how you feel about something, and
- tells why you feel that way.

6 Write an Opinion Paragraph

Instruct students to complete the writing assignment independently, with a partner, or in small groups.

If needed, review the structure of an opinion paragraph:

- The topic sentence tells your opinion about the subject.
- Detail sentences give reasons that support your opinion.

Name ________________________________

UNIT 13

Thurgood Marshall

Unit Focus

You are going to read a biography of Thurgood Marshall.

As You Read:

Think about how Thurgood Marshall helped others and our country.

After You Read:

Use information from the biography to write an opinion paragraph about Thurgood Marshall's work.

Lesson Checklist

Check off each task after you complete it.

- [ ] **Learn Vocabulary**
- [ ] **Read the Biography: *Thurgood Marshall***
- [ ] **Answer Questions About the Biography**
- [ ] **Organize Information**
- [ ] **Write an Opinion Paragraph**

Name ______________________________

UNIT 13

Thurgood Marshall

Learn Vocabulary

Look at the pictures. Read the words.

Read the word and write it on the line.
Then read the Words to Know.

Content Words

court ______________________

Constitution ______________________

lawyer ______________________

segregation ______________________

Words to Know

equal separated

rights unfair

Name ______________________________

Thurgood Marshall

Thurgood Marshall was born in 1908. Life was very different when Marshall was growing up. Back then, black and white people were separated. They could not eat at the same restaurants or go to the same schools. This was called segregation. Marshall thought black people should have the same rights as white people.

Marshall became a lawyer. He read the Constitution carefully. The Fourteenth Amendment said that all people should have equal rights. In the 1930s, Marshall started fighting for those rights. He traveled around the country to help black people fight against segregation.

In 1953, Marshall went to the United States Supreme Court. He brought a case called "Brown versus the Board of Education." Marshall argued that segregated schools were not equal. He showed the court that the schools were unfair. Black teachers and students were not getting enough money or supplies. White teachers and students were getting a lot of these things. The Supreme Court agreed with Marshall. They said segregation was unfair and unequal. Marshall won the case.

In 1967, Marshall became a judge on the Supreme Court. He was the first black judge on the court, which makes him a very important person in American history. He worked hard to make life right for many people. He left the court in 1991 and died in 1993. Marshall spent his whole life working to make this country a better place to live.

Name ____________________

UNIT 13

Thurgood Marshall

Answer Questions

1. Thurgood Marshall traveled around the country to ___.

   Ⓐ learn more about the Constitution

   Ⓑ help black people fight against segregation

   Ⓒ make sure blacks and whites were kept separate

2. Marshall went to the Supreme Court in 1953 to ___.

   Ⓐ become a lawyer

   Ⓑ fight for equal rights

   Ⓒ work as a judge

3. Draw a picture of Thurgood Marshall as a judge.

Name ______________________________

UNIT 13

Thurgood Marshall

Organize Information

Read the biography again. Then write your opinion about **Thurgood Marshall's work**. Did he help other people and our country? Next, write reasons from the biography that support your opinion.

Opinion

Reasons (Why?)

Name ____________________

UNIT 13

Thurgood Marshall

Opinion

Write a paragraph that tells your opinion about **Thurgood Marshall's work**. Did he help others and make this country better? Why or why not?

- Use information from your graphic organizer and the biography.

____
Title

Jane Goodall

Lesson Objectives

Writing
Students use information from the biography to write an opinion paragraph.

Vocabulary
Students learn content vocabulary words and use those words to write about how Jane Goodall helps chimpanzees.

Content Knowledge
Students understand that Jane Goodall brings awareness to chimpanzees and their struggles.

Essential Understanding
Students understand that animals are important to people and to the world.

Prepare

Reproduce and distribute one copy for each student.

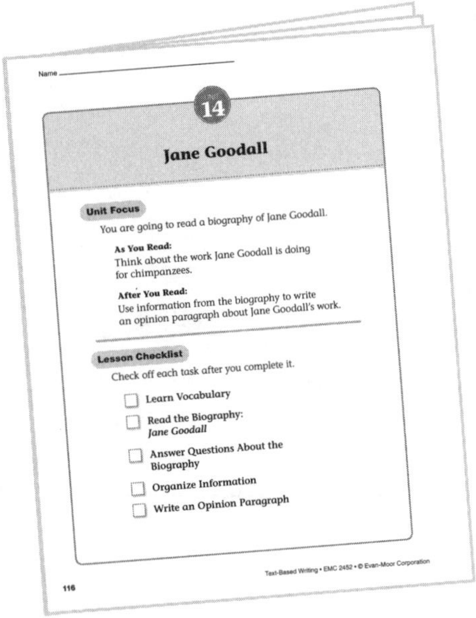
Name

14

Jane Goodall

Unit Focus
You are going to read a biography of Jane Goodall.
As You Read:
Think about the work Jane Goodall is doing for chimpanzees.
After You Read:
Use information from the biography to write an opinion paragraph about Jane Goodall's work.

Lesson Checklist
Check off each task after you complete it.
☐ Learn Vocabulary
☐ Read the Biography: *Jane Goodall*
☐ Answer Questions About the Biography
☐ Organize Information
☐ Write an Opinion Paragraph

116 Text-Based Writing • EMC 2452 • © Evan-Moor Corporation

1 Unit Focus and Lesson Checklist

Distribute one unit to each student and direct students' attention to the Unit Focus and Lesson Checklist. Tell them they will be able to refer to the focus of the unit as needed while working on the lessons. Instruct students to check off each task on the checklist after they complete it.

Read aloud the focus statements, and verify that students understand their purpose for reading. Ask:

- *Who are we going to read about?* (Jane Goodall)
- *What are you going to learn about her?* (her work for chimpanzees)
- *What are you going to write based on this biography?* (an opinion paragraph)

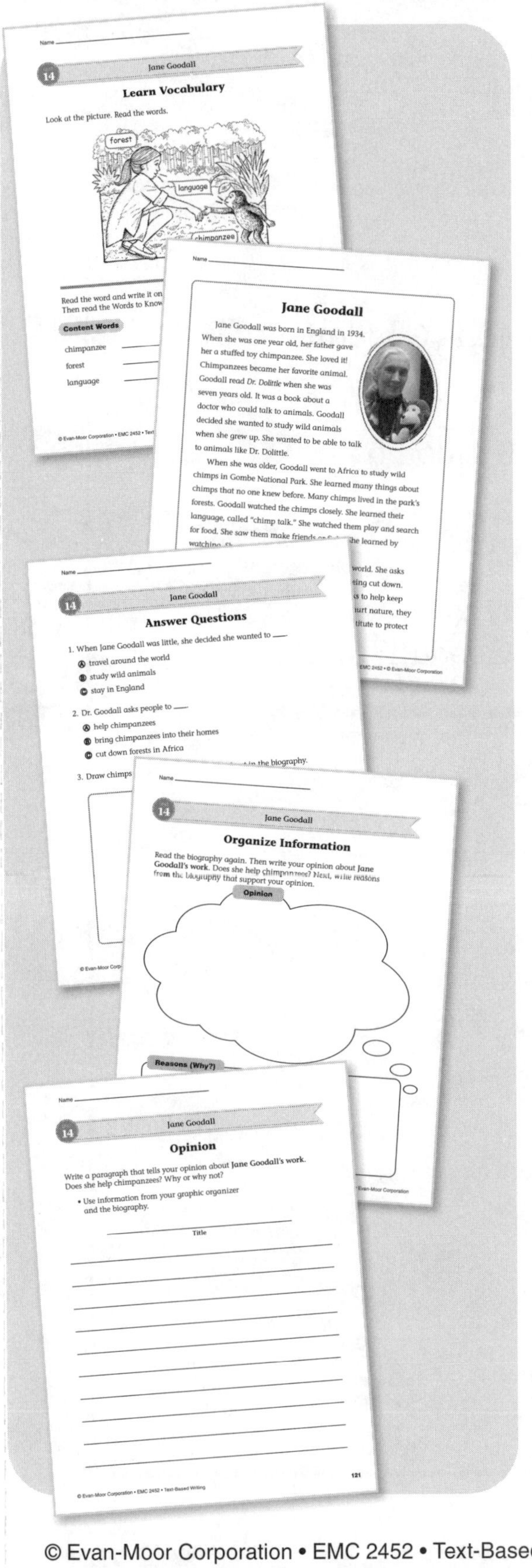

2 Learn Vocabulary

Direct students' attention to the picture dictionary. Read aloud each content vocabulary word and have students repeat. Point out that the words are related to Jane Goodall's work and that students will have a better understanding of the words after they read the biography. Have students write the vocabulary words on the provided lines. Then review the Words to Know, and encourage students to ask questions about any words they do not understand.

3 Read the Biography: *Jane Goodall*

Read aloud the biography as students follow along silently. Then have students reread the biography independently or in small groups.

4 Answer Questions About the Biography

To ensure reading comprehension, have students answer the text-dependent questions. Review the answers together.

5 Organize Information

Explain to students that they will use an opinion graphic organizer to help them plan their paragraphs. Guide students in using the text to complete the organizer, rereading the biography if needed.

Remind students that an opinion paragraph:

- tells how you feel about something, and
- tells why you feel that way.

6 Write an Opinion Paragraph

Instruct students to complete the writing assignment independently, with a partner, or in small groups.

If needed, review the structure of an opinion paragraph:

- The topic sentence tells your opinion about the subject.
- Detail sentences give reasons that support your opinion.

Name ______________________________

UNIT 14

Jane Goodall

Unit Focus

You are going to read a biography of Jane Goodall.

As You Read:
Think about the work Jane Goodall is doing for chimpanzees.

After You Read:
Use information from the biography to write an opinion paragraph about Jane Goodall's work.

Lesson Checklist

Check off each task after you complete it.

- ☐ **Learn Vocabulary**
- ☐ **Read the Biography: *Jane Goodall***
- ☐ **Answer Questions About the Biography**
- ☐ **Organize Information**
- ☐ **Write an Opinion Paragraph**

Name ______________________________

UNIT 14

Jane Goodall

Learn Vocabulary

Look at the picture. Read the words.

Read the word and write it on the line.
Then read the Words to Know.

Content Words

chimpanzee ____________________

forest ____________________

language ____________________

Words to Know

doctor	learned
environment	search
fight	watch
hunt	wild

Name ___________________________

Jane Goodall

Jane Goodall was born in England in 1934. When she was one year old, her father gave her a stuffed toy chimpanzee. She loved it! Chimpanzees became her favorite animal. Goodall read *Dr. Dolittle* when she was seven years old. It was a book about a doctor who could talk to animals. Goodall decided she wanted to study wild animals when she grew up. She wanted to be able to talk to animals like Dr. Dolittle.

When she was older, Goodall went to Africa to study wild chimps in Gombe National Park. She learned many things about chimps that no one knew before. Many chimps lived in the park's forests. Goodall watched the chimps closely. She learned their language, called "chimp talk." She watched them play and search for food. She saw them make friends or fight. She learned by watching. She told people what she learned.

Today, Dr. Jane Goodall travels all over the world. She asks people to help chimpanzees. Many forests are being cut down. Some people hunt chimps for food. Goodall works to help keep chimps safe. Goodall believes that when people hurt nature, they hurt themselves. She started the Jane Goodall Institute to protect chimpanzees and their environments.

Name ____

UNIT 14

Jane Goodall

Answer Questions

1. When Jane Goodall was little, she decided she wanted to ___.

   Ⓐ travel around the world

   Ⓑ study wild animals

   Ⓒ stay in England

2. Dr. Goodall asks people to ___.

   Ⓐ help chimpanzees

   Ⓑ bring chimpanzees into their homes

   Ⓒ cut down forests in Africa

3. Draw chimps doing something you read about in the biography.

Name ______________________________

UNIT 14 Jane Goodall

Organize Information

Read the biography again. Then write your opinion about **Jane Goodall's work**. Does she help chimpanzees? Next, write reasons from the biography that support your opinion.

Opinion

Reasons (Why?)

Name ____________________________________

UNIT 14

Jane Goodall

Opinion

Write a paragraph that tells your opinion about **Jane Goodall's work**. Does she help chimpanzees? Why or why not?

- Use information from your graphic organizer and the biography.

____

Title

____

____

____

____

____

____

____

____

____

____

UNIT 15

Social Studies Article – Level L

Opinion Letter Writing Prompt

Presidents in the Mountain

Lesson Objectives

Writing
Students use information from the social studies article to write a letter.

Vocabulary
Students learn content vocabulary words and use those words to explain why their class should take a trip.

Content Knowledge
Students understand that Mount Rushmore is an important historic place.

Essential Understanding
Students understand that they can learn American history by visiting places such as Mount Rushmore.

Prepare

Reproduce and distribute one copy for each student.

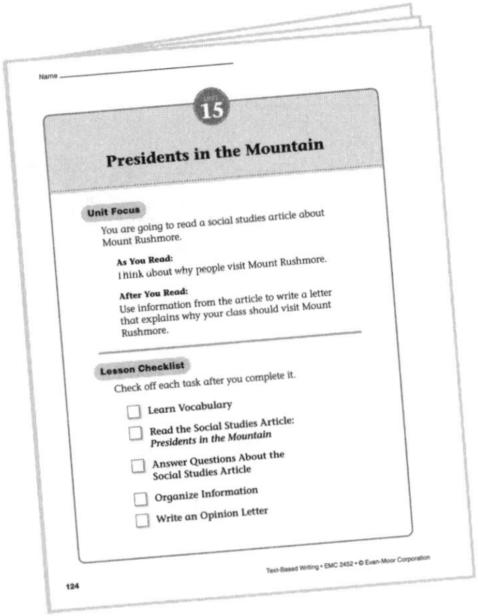
Name

UNIT 15

Presidents in the Mountain

Unit Focus
You are going to read a social studies article about Mount Rushmore.

As You Read:
Think about why people visit Mount Rushmore.

After You Read:
Use information from the article to write a letter that explains why your class should visit Mount Rushmore.

Lesson Checklist
Check off each task after you complete it.

- [ ] Learn Vocabulary
- [ ] Read the Social Studies Article: *Presidents in the Mountain*
- [ ] Answer Questions About the Social Studies Article
- [ ] Organize Information
- [ ] Write an Opinion Letter

124

Text-Based Writing • EMC 2452 • © Evan-Moor Corporation

1 Unit Focus and Lesson Checklist

Distribute one unit to each student and direct students' attention to the Unit Focus and Lesson Checklist. Tell them they will be able to refer to the focus of the unit as needed while working on the lessons. Instruct students to check off each task on the checklist after they complete it.

Read aloud the focus statements, and verify that students understand their purpose for reading. Ask:

- *What are we going to read about?* (Mount Rushmore)
- *What are you going to learn about it?* (why people visit there)
- *What are you going to write based on this article?* (an opinion letter)

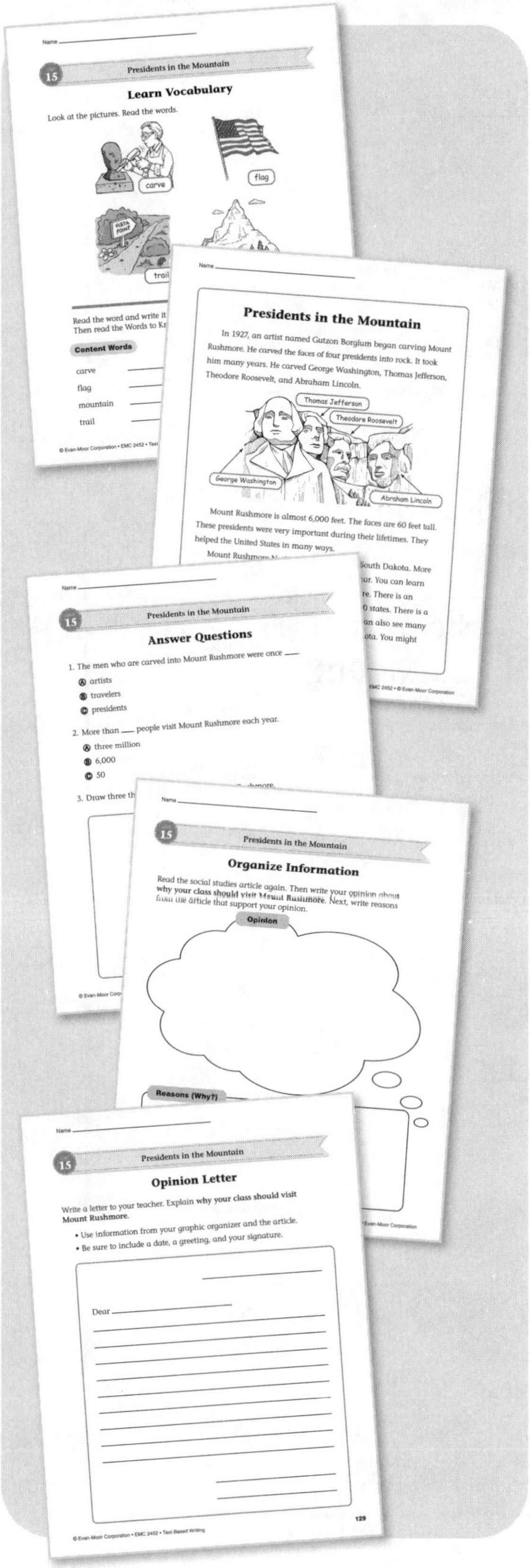

2 Learn Vocabulary

Direct students' attention to the picture dictionary. Read aloud each content vocabulary word and have students repeat. Point out that the words are related to Mount Rushmore and that students will have a better understanding of the words after they read the social studies article. Have students write the vocabulary words on the provided lines. Then review the Words to Know, and encourage students to ask questions about any words they do not understand.

3 Read the Social Studies Article: *Presidents in the Mountain*

Read aloud the social studies article as students follow along silently. Then have students reread the article independently or in small groups.

4 Answer Questions About the Social Studies Article

To ensure reading comprehension, have students answer the text-dependent questions. Review the answers together.

5 Organize Information

Explain to students that they will use a graphic organizer to help them plan their letters. Guide students in using the text to complete the organizer, rereading the article if needed.

Remind students that a letter:

- is sent from you to another person, and
- shares a message or a request.

6 Write an Opinion Letter

Instruct students to complete the writing assignment independently, with a partner, or in small groups.

If needed, review the structure of a letter:

- It includes a date, a greeting, a message, and a signature.
- It tells why you are writing to the person.

Name ________________________________

UNIT 15

Presidents in the Mountain

Unit Focus

You are going to read a social studies article about Mount Rushmore.

As You Read:
Think about why people visit Mount Rushmore.

After You Read:
Use information from the article to write a letter that explains why your class should visit Mount Rushmore.

Lesson Checklist

Check off each task after you complete it.

- [ ] **Learn Vocabulary**
- [ ] **Read the Social Studies Article: *Presidents in the Mountain***
- [ ] **Answer Questions About the Social Studies Article**
- [ ] **Organize Information**
- [ ] **Write an Opinion Letter**

Name ______________________________

UNIT 15

Presidents in the Mountain

Learn Vocabulary

Look at the pictures. Read the words.

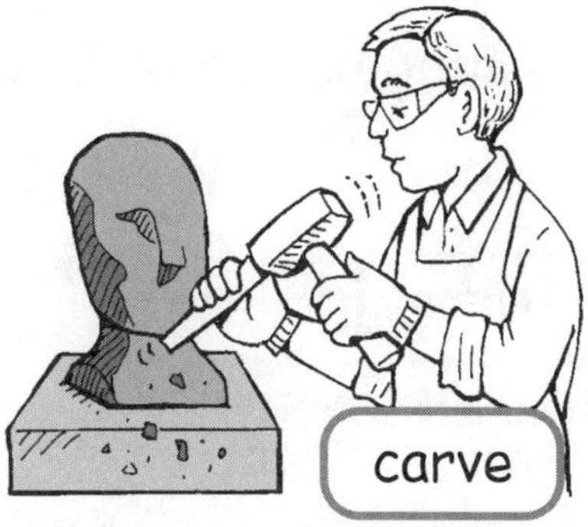

Read the word and write it on the line.
Then read the Words to Know.

Content Words

carve ______________

flag ______________

mountain ______________

trail ______________

Words to Know

artist
memorial
avenue
president
lifetime

Name ______________________________

Presidents in the Mountain

In 1927, an artist named Gutzon Borglum began carving Mount Rushmore. He carved the faces of four presidents into rock. It took him many years. He carved George Washington, Thomas Jefferson, Theodore Roosevelt, and Abraham Lincoln.

Mount Rushmore is almost 6,000 feet. The faces are 60 feet tall. These presidents were very important during their lifetimes. They helped the United States in many ways.

Mount Rushmore National Memorial is in South Dakota. More than three million people visit the area each year. You can learn a lot about American history at Mount Rushmore. There is an Avenue of Flags. It has one flag for each of the 50 states. There is a Presidential Trail that you can walk along. You can also see many plants, animals, and birds that live in South Dakota. You might even see a bald eagle!

Name ___________________________

UNIT 15

Presidents in the Mountain

Answer Questions

1. The men who are carved into Mount Rushmore were once ____.

   Ⓐ artists

   Ⓑ travelers

   Ⓒ presidents

2. More than ____ people visit Mount Rushmore each year.

   Ⓐ three million

   Ⓑ 6,000

   Ⓒ 50

3. Draw three things you could see at Mount Rushmore.

Name ______________________________

UNIT 15 Presidents in the Mountain

Organize Information

Read the social studies article again. Then write your opinion about **why your class should visit Mount Rushmore**. Next, write reasons from the article that support your opinion.

Opinion

Reasons (Why?)

Name ______________________________

UNIT 15 Presidents in the Mountain

Opinion Letter

Write a letter to your teacher. Explain **why your class should visit Mount Rushmore.**

- Use information from your graphic organizer and the article.
- Be sure to include a date, a greeting, and your signature.

Dear ______________________________,

Answer Key

Unit 1

1 Lakes and Oceans

Answer Questions

1. Earth's oceans have ___.
   - ● salt water
   - Ⓑ small amounts of water
   - Ⓒ land all around them
2. Lakes have ___.
   - Ⓐ salt water
   - Ⓑ small amounts of water
   - ● fresh water
3. Think about what you read. Draw a picture of one of the things people do in the Earth's oceans. Write a sentence to go with your picture.

Answers will vary.

Page 15

1 Lakes and Oceans

Organize Information

Read the geography article again. Then write information in the graphic organizer that tells **how lakes and oceans are alike and different.**

Lakes
- fresh water
- land all around them
- thousands on Earth
- people and animals can drink

Both
- hold most of the water on Earth
- plants and animals live in them

Oceans
- salt water
- five oceans on Earth
- people cannot drink salt water
- travel across to get to different countries

Page 16

Unit 2

2 Owl Facts

Answer Questions

1. One way owls are alike is that they all ___.
   - Ⓐ have extra feathers on their legs
   - Ⓑ make their nests in barns
   - ● have sharp claws on their feet
2. Barn owls are different from snowy owls because barn owls ___.
   - ● have faces that are shaped like hearts
   - Ⓑ have extra padding on their feet
   - Ⓒ can't move their eyes like humans can
3. Draw a picture of a snowy owl in its nest. Then draw a barn owl in its nest. Label each part of your pictures.

Answers will vary.

Page 23

2 Owl Facts

Organize Information

Read the science article again. Then write information in the graphic organizer that tells **how snowy owls and barn owls are alike and different.**

Snowy Owls
- white
- more feathers on legs and feet
- feet have extra padding
- make low hooting sounds
- most live in Arctic
- nests are on the ground

Both
- large heads
- circles of feathers around eyes
- can't move their eyes like humans
- sharp claws on feet

Barn Owls
- face looks like a heart
- bodies are small, wings are large
- light gray with spots
- make hissing or screeching sound
- hunt for food only at night
- make nests in holes, buildings, barns

Page 24

Unit 3

3 Beavers at Work

Answer Questions

1. Beavers can change a stream by ___.
   - ● building a dam
   - Ⓑ scooping mud with their claws
   - Ⓒ moving to a new location
2. Beavers build lodges so they can ___.
   - Ⓐ create new ponds
   - ● live inside them
   - Ⓒ keep water out
3. Draw a picture of a beaver working on its lodge.

Answers will vary.

Page 31

3 Beavers at Work

Organize Information

Read the science article again. Then write information in the graphic organizer that tells **how beavers build lodges from start to finish.**

Start: They use their sharp front teeth to cut wood.

They push wood through the water to the lodge area where they stack the wood.

They use their claws to scoop up mud and grass.

Finish: They pack mud and grass on top of the lodge to hold the sticks together.

Page 32

Unit 4

4 The Life of a Worker Bee

Answer Questions

1. The first thing a worker bee does is ___.
   - Ⓐ go out to get food
   - ● clean the cell where it was born
   - Ⓒ make royal jelly for the queen
2. Worker bees use ___ to make cells.
   - Ⓐ eggs
   - Ⓑ honey
   - ● wax
3. Draw a picture of a worker bee flying away from its hive. Show where it is going.

Answers will vary.

Page 39

4 The Life of a Worker Bee

Organize Information

Read the science article again. Then write information in the graphic organizer that tells **the jobs a worker bee has as it grows.**

Job 1: It cleans the cell where it was born.

Job 2: It makes worker jelly to feed new babies. It also makes royal jelly for the queen.

Job 3: It makes wax to build new cells.

Job 4: It looks for food in flowers and fields. It brings food back to the hive. It turns food into honey.

Page 40

Unit 5

5 Community Helpers

Answer Questions

1. Community helpers work to help their community's ___.
   - ● citizens
   - Ⓑ firefighters
   - Ⓒ packages
2. Police officers work to ___.
   - Ⓐ deliver mail
   - Ⓑ teach about fire safety
   - ● keep people safe
3. Draw a picture of your favorite community helper.

Answers will vary.

Page 47

5 Community Helpers

Organize Information

Read the social studies article again. Then write information in the graphic organizer that tells **the important jobs community helpers do.**

Community Helpers
- Firefighters put out fires. They rescue people or animals.
- Postal workers deliver letters and packages. They collect mail and bring it to the post office.
- Police officers keep people safe. They make sure people follow laws.
- Bus drivers take people to places around town.

Page 48

Unit 6

6 One Milk, Please

Answer Questions

1. Milk is a ___.
   - Ⓐ dairy food
   - Ⓑ good choice
   - ● both A and B
2. Milk protects new babies from ___.
   - Ⓐ growing bigger
   - ● getting sick
   - Ⓒ getting too much calcium
3. Draw two foods you like to eat from the dairy food group.

Answers will vary.

Page 55

6 One Milk, Please

Organize Information

Read the health article again. Then write information in the graphic organizer that tells **why milk is important for humans.**

Milk
- Milk is good for your body.
- Milk has a lot of calcium. It helps your bones grow.
- Milk helps babies grow. It protects them from getting sick.
- Milk keeps your blood healthy.

Page 56

Unit 7

Name ___

7 The Great Lakes

Answer Questions

1. Lake Michigan and Lake Huron both ___.
   - Ⓐ are 802 feet deep
   - ● bend around Michigan
   - Ⓒ touch Canada
2. The Great Lakes are in the ___ part of the United States.
   - ● northeast
   - Ⓑ southern
   - Ⓒ western
3. Draw the five Great Lakes. Write the name of each lake next to its picture.

Answers will vary.

© Evan-Moor Corporation • EMC 2452 • Text-Based Writing 63

Page 63

Name ___

7 The Great Lakes

Organize Information

Read the geography article again. Then write in the graphic organizer **two facts about the Great Lakes and one fact about each lake.**

The Great Lakes

- **Fact 1:** They are in the northeast part of the country.
- **Fact 2:** They are 5 lakes with fresh water that are extra large.

- **Lake Superior:** Largest, deepest, and coldest of the lakes
- **Lake Michigan:** People like to go to its sandy shores
- **Lake Huron:** Looks like it could be two different lakes
- **Lake Erie:** Gets water from 3 other lakes
- **Lake Ontario:** The smallest lake, but it is very deep

64 Text-Based Writing • EMC 2452 • © Evan-Moor Corporation

Page 64

Unit 8

Name ___

8 Another Cold!

Answer Questions

1. People get more colds in the winter because ___.
   - Ⓐ they are coughing and sneezing
   - Ⓑ cold germs like cold weather
   - ● they share more germs
2. You can stay healthy by ___.
   - ● washing your hands
   - Ⓑ going inside
   - Ⓒ touching your eyes
3. Draw two things you use in your classroom. Could cold germs get on these things? Write *yes* or *no* beside each picture.

Answers will vary.

© Evan-Moor Corporation • EMC 2452 • Text-Based Writing 71

Page 71

Name ___

8 Another Cold!

Organize Information

Read the health article again. Then write information in the graphic organizer that tells **how people get colds.** Think about what happens (effect) and why it happens (cause).

Cause	Effect
People are close together in a room	they share germs
Cold germs get into your body	your body tries to get rid of germs by coughing or sneezing
If you can't get the germs out	you will get sick
People cough or sneeze	the germs get on other people
Wash your hands with warm water and soap	cold germs will be killed

72 Text-Based Writing • EMC 2452 • © Evan-Moor Corporation

Page 72

Unit 9

Name ___

9 Earthworms in the Garden

Answer Questions

1. The bristles on an earthworm's segments help it to ___.
   - ● hold onto the soil as it moves through it
   - Ⓑ eat dead leaves and plant bits
   - Ⓒ stay dry when it rains
2. The piles that earthworms leave behind after they have eaten ___.
   - Ⓐ are easy to see after it rains
   - Ⓑ are called burrows
   - ● give the soil nutrients
3. Draw a picture of an earthworm moving through soil.

Answers will vary.

© Evan-Moor Corporation • EMC 2452 • Text-Based Writing 79

Page 79

Name ___

9 Earthworms in the Garden

Organize Information

Read the science article again. Then write information in the graphic organizer that tells **how earthworms change the soil** (cause) **and help a garden grow** (effect).

Cause	Effect
Earthworms dig large burrows	burrows let water and air into the soil
Earthworms eat dead leaves and plant bits	the food passes through worm's body and is left in piles on the ground
The soil gets nutrients from the piles	the piles help plants grow

80 Text-Based Writing • EMC 2452 • © Evan-Moor Corporation

Page 80

Unit 10

Name ___

10 Let's Work Together!

Answer Questions

1. A team is made up of ___.
   - Ⓐ school sports
   - Ⓑ adults
   - ● two or more people
2. When you are a part of a team, you have to ___.
   - Ⓐ play a sport
   - ● think of others
   - Ⓒ work at a school
3. Draw a picture of your favorite sports team.

Answers will vary.

© Evan-Moor Corporation • EMC 2452 • Text-Based Writing 87

Page 87

Name ___

10 Let's Work Together!

Organize Information

Read the social studies article again. Then write your opinion about **how playing on a sports team will or will not help you in the future.** Next, write reasons from the social studies article that support your opinion.

Opinion: I think playing on a sports team will help me in the future.

Reasons (Why?)

- Playing on a sports team will teach me how to work together with others.
- I will learn to think of others.
- I will learn how to be a good team member.

88 Text-Based Writing • EMC 2452 • © Evan-Moor Corporation

Page 88

Unit 11

Name ___

11 Too Much Garbage

Answer Questions

1. Trash is a problem because it can ___.
   - Ⓐ be covered with soil
   - Ⓑ stay in garbage cans
   - ● hurt the ground and people
2. Which of these can you reuse while shopping?
   - Ⓐ paper
   - Ⓑ a plastic cup
   - ● a cloth bag
3. Draw something you can reuse instead of throwing it away.

Answers will vary.

© Evan-Moor Corporation • EMC 2452 • Text-Based Writing 95

Page 95

Name ___

11 Too Much Garbage

Organize Information

Read the social studies article again. Then write information in the graphic organizer that tells about the **problem of too much garbage and the solutions to this problem.**

Problem	Solution
There is too much garbage.	Send less trash to the landfill.
Each person makes 4 pounds of garbage each day.	Recycle plastic, paper, and glass.
Most trash goes to landfills.	Reuse bags, cups, and paper to make less trash.
It hurts the ground and nature.	

96 Text-Based Writing • EMC 2452 • © Evan-Moor Corporation

Page 96

Unit 12

Name ___

12 Washington's Barn

Answer Questions

1. George Washington had a problem with ___.
   - ● getting wheat kernels off the stalks
   - Ⓑ cutting wheat stalks in the fields
   - Ⓒ sweeping up wheat kernels in the barn
2. Washington's barn made it ___ to make flour.
   - Ⓐ harder
   - ● easier
   - Ⓒ healthier
3. Draw a picture of a horse walking on wheat stalks.

Answers will vary.

© Evan-Moor Corporation • EMC 2452 • Text-Based Writing 103

Page 103

Name ___

12 Washington's Barn

Organize Information

Read the social studies article again. Then write information in the graphic organizer that tells about **George Washington's problem and solution.**

Problem	Solution
Getting wheat kernels off the wheat stalks was hard.	Washington built a barn with levels.
It took too much time.	Horses walked on the wheat stalks.
	Wheat kernels fell through the holes.
	Workers swept up the kernels.

104 Text-Based Writing • EMC 2452 • © Evan-Moor Corporation

Page 104

Unit 13

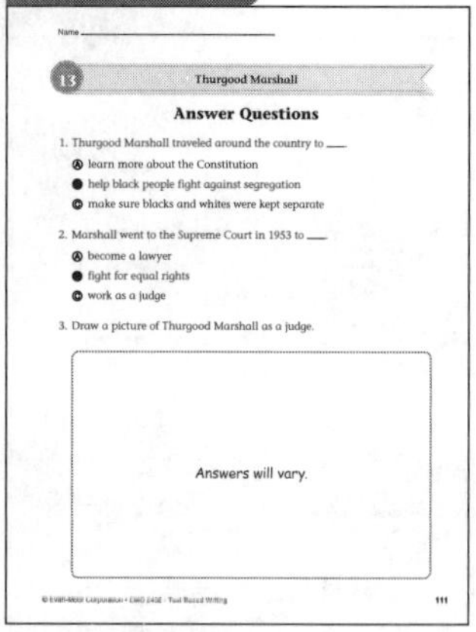
Name ____________

13 Thurgood Marshall

Answer Questions

1. Thurgood Marshall traveled around the country to ___
   - Ⓐ learn more about the Constitution
   - ● help black people fight against segregation
   - Ⓒ make sure blacks and whites were kept separate
2. Marshall went to the Supreme Court in 1953 to ___
   - Ⓐ become a lawyer
   - ● fight for equal rights
   - Ⓒ work as a judge
3. Draw a picture of Thurgood Marshall as a judge.

Answers will vary.

Page 111

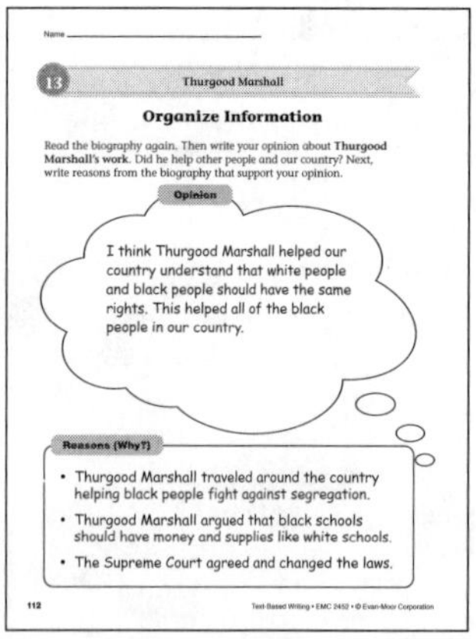
Name ____________

13 Thurgood Marshall

Organize Information

Read the biography again. Then write your opinion about **Thurgood Marshall's work**. Did he help other people and our country? Next, write reasons from the biography that support your opinion.

Opinion

I think Thurgood Marshall helped our country understand that white people and black people should have the same rights. This helped all of the black people in our country.

Reasons (Why?)

- Thurgood Marshall traveled around the country helping black people fight against segregation.
- Thurgood Marshall argued that black schools should have money and supplies like white schools.
- The Supreme Court agreed and changed the laws.

Page 112

Unit 14

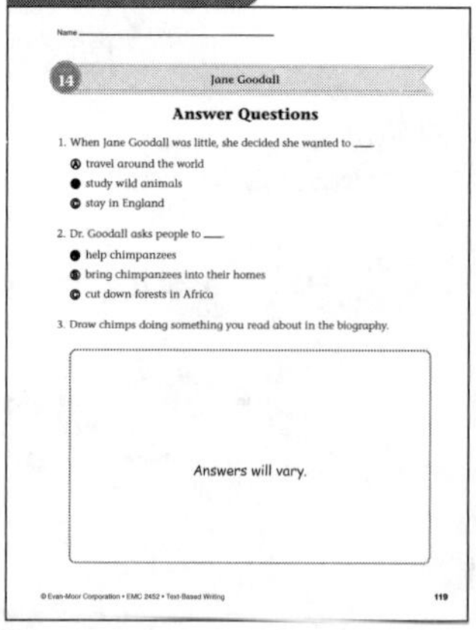
Name ____________

14 Jane Goodall

Answer Questions

1. When Jane Goodall was little, she decided she wanted to ___
   - Ⓐ travel around the world
   - ● study wild animals
   - Ⓒ stay in England
2. Dr. Goodall asks people to ___
   - ● help chimpanzees
   - Ⓑ bring chimpanzees into their homes
   - Ⓒ cut down forests in Africa
3. Draw chimps doing something you read about in the biography.

Answers will vary.

Page 119

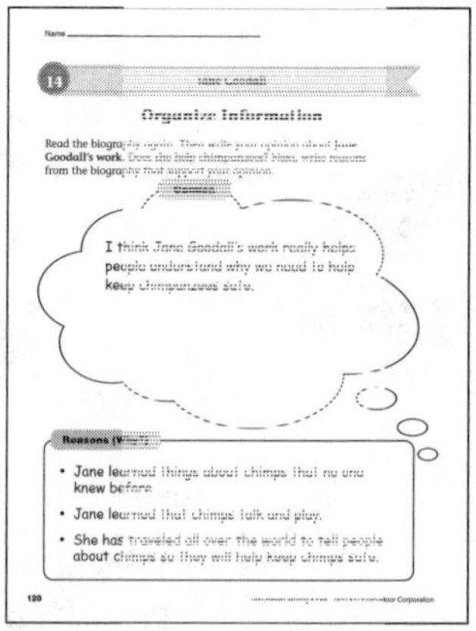
Name ____________

14 Jane Goodall

Organize Information

Read the biography again. Then write your opinion about **Jane Goodall's work**. Does she help chimpanzees? Next, write reasons from the biography that support your opinion.

Opinion

I think Jane Goodall's work really helps people understand why we need to help keep chimpanzees safe.

Reasons (Why?)

- Jane learned things about chimps that no one knew before.
- Jane learned that chimps talk and play.
- She has traveled all over the world to tell people about chimps so they will help keep chimps safe.

Page 120

Unit 15

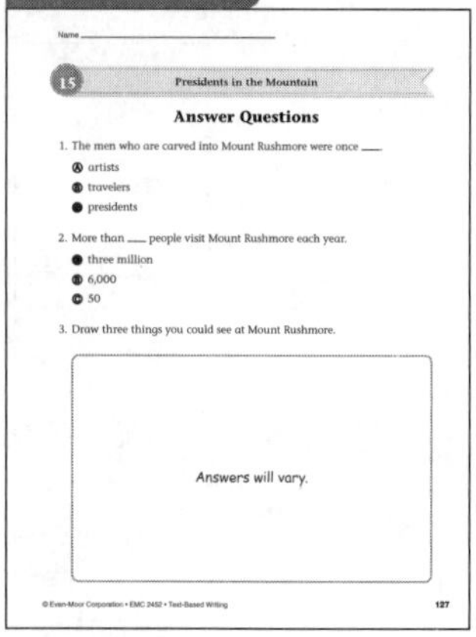
Name ____________

15 Presidents in the Mountain

Answer Questions

1. The men who are carved into Mount Rushmore were once ___
   - Ⓐ artists
   - Ⓑ travelers
   - ● presidents
2. More than ___ people visit Mount Rushmore each year.
   - ● three million
   - Ⓑ 6,000
   - Ⓒ 50
3. Draw three things you could see at Mount Rushmore.

Answers will vary.

Page 127

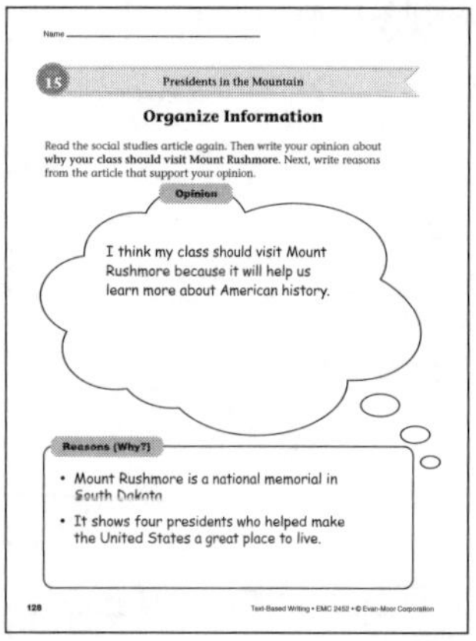
Name ____________

15 Presidents in the Mountain

Organize Information

Read the social studies article again. Then write your opinion about **why your class should visit Mount Rushmore**. Next, write reasons from the article that support your opinion.

Opinion

I think my class should visit Mount Rushmore because it will help us learn more about American history.

Reasons (Why?)

- Mount Rushmore is a national memorial in South Dakota.
- It shows four presidents who helped make the United States a great place to live.

Page 128

Reading Comprehension Nonfiction

Grade 2

SAMPLER

LEVEL I

Science

Baby Blue Whale

Lesson Objective Students will learn about how baby blue whales grow, eat, and breathe like their parents.

Content Knowledge Animals have a life cycle and traits like their parents.

Lesson Preparation

Reproduce and distribute to each student one copy of the dictionary page (p. 15), the student text (p. 16), and the activity pages (pp. 17–21).

Learn

1. Build Background
2. Introduce the Vocabulary
   Dictionary
3. Read the Texts
   Baby Blue Whale
   Teacher's Complex Text

Analyze

4. Reading Comprehension Activities
   I Read and Understand
   I Read Closely
5. Close Reading Activity
   Oral Discussion Questions
6. Vocabulary Activity
   Words I Know

Write

7. Writing Activities
   I Can Write
   What I Learned

1 Build Background

Explain to students that baby animals have many different names. For example, the name for a baby cow, elephant, giraffe, or whale is *calf.* Explain that baby animals grow up to look and act the same as their parents.

2 Introduce the Vocabulary

Content Vocabulary Point to each pictured word. Read the word aloud and have students echo you. Then have them write the word on the line. Explain phonetic structures that are unfamiliar to students. Point out the silent letters in *calf* and *comb.* Discuss word meanings as needed.

Words to Know Point to each word and read it aloud. Have students echo you. Point out the following:

- The letters *ea* in *breath* have a short sound: /ĕ/.
- The letters *ea* in *breathe* have a long sound: /ē/.
- A *mist* is made up of tiny water droplets floating in air.
- The word *surface* is a multiple-meaning word. In this text, *surface* means "the top of the ocean water where there is air to breathe."

3 Read the Texts

Student Text Guide students in reading the text together aloud. Then have them retell the main idea and give details they learned about whales from the text.

Teacher's Complex Text Have students look at the picture in their text and listen as you read aloud the Teacher's Complex Text on page 14. Say: *Look at the picture and listen as I read more information about the baby blue whale.*

4 Reading Comprehension Activities

Guide students through completing the activities on pages 17 and 18. Encourage them to look at their text to find information.

5 Close Reading Activity

Oral Discussion Use the Oral Discussion Questions on the right to guide students in a discussion about what they have read and heard. Before you begin, make sure each student has colored pencils and his or her text.

Begin by reading aloud a question. Then have students answer the question and mark the answer in their text.

6 Vocabulary Activity

Review the vocabulary on the *Dictionary* page. Then guide students through the *Words I Know* activity.

7 Writing Activities

Guide students through the first writing activity, *I Can Write*. Then have them read aloud their facts and discuss their pictures with a partner. Discuss the writing prompt on the second writing page, *What I Learned*. As an informal assessment of students' understanding of the topic, have them write their paragraphs independently.

Oral Discussion Questions

1. **Why did the author write this text?** (*It was written to tell facts about baby blue whales.*) **Make a blue dot next to your favorite fact about baby blue whales.**

2. **What facts explain how a baby blue whale grows, breathes, and eats like its parents?** (*They are very large; they grow fast; they breathe air; they eat krill.*) **Draw a green line under the key words that tell about these traits.**

3. **How does a blue whale's baleen work? Explain how a blue whale eats.** (*The whale takes a huge gulp of water. The baleen lets the water escape, but keeps the krill for the whale to eat.*) **Make a red X next to the paragraph that tells about baleen.**

4. **Look at the picture in your text. Why does the mother blue whale push her calf up to the surface of the water after it is born?** (*The mother whale pushes her calf up to the surface so that it can get its first breath of air; it needs to breathe air.*) **Draw a purple line under the key words that tell about this.**

5. **Put your finger on a word that you didn't know.** (*E.g., krill*) **Draw a yellow line under the word. What clues in the text helped you figure out what the word means?** (*Answers will vary.*)

6. **Adult blue whales are about 100 feet long. Tell what the author compared the blue whale's size to.** (*Adult blue whales are about as long as three school buses.*)

Baby Blue Whale

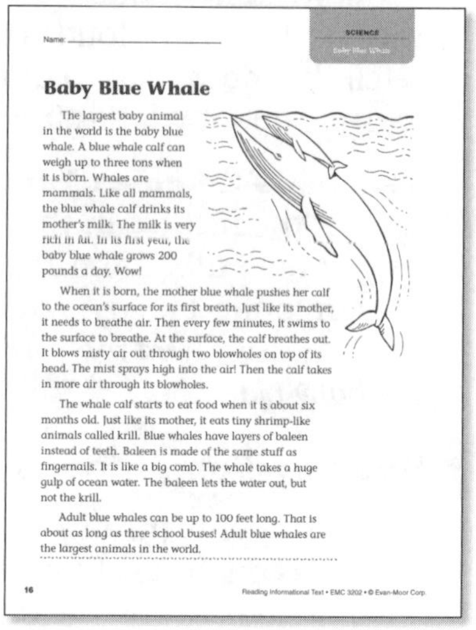

Name: __________

SCIENCE

Baby Blue Whale

The largest baby animal in the world is the baby blue whale. A blue whale calf can weigh up to three tons when it is born. Whales are mammals. Like all mammals, the blue whale calf drinks its mother's milk. The milk is very rich in fat. In its first year, the baby blue whale grows 200 pounds a day. Wow!

When it is born, the mother blue whale pushes her calf to the ocean's surface for its first breath. Just like its mother, it needs to breathe air. Then every few minutes, it swims to the surface to breathe. At the surface, the calf breathes out. It blows misty air out through two blowholes on top of its head. The mist sprays high into the air! Then the calf takes in more air through its blowholes.

The whale calf starts to eat food when it is about six months old. Just like its mother, it eats tiny shrimp-like animals called krill. Blue whales have layers of baleen instead of teeth. Baleen is made of the same stuff as fingernails. It is like a big comb. The whale takes a huge gulp of ocean water. The baleen lets the water out, but not the krill.

Adult blue whales can be up to 100 feet long. That is about as long as three school buses! Adult blue whales are the largest animals in the world.

16 Reading Informational Text • EMC 3202 • © Evan-Moor Corp.

student text, p. 16

The largest baby animal in the world is the baby blue whale. Another name for a baby whale is a calf. A blue whale calf can weigh up to three tons when it is born. Whales are mammals, which means they are warm-blooded and breathe air. Like all mammals, a whale calf drinks its mother's milk. The milk is very rich in fat. In its first year, the baby blue whale grows 200 pounds a day. Wow! It is the fastest-growing animal baby on Earth.

When it is born, the mother guides the calf to take its first breath. She pushes her baby to the surface of the water. Just like its mother, the baby whale needs to breathe air. Because it cannot breathe underwater, it must swim to the surface every few minutes. The blue whale calf has two blowholes on the top of its head, instead of nostrils, for breathing. It blows out misty air through the blowholes. The mist sprays high into the air! Then the calf takes in fresh air.

The blue whale calf starts to eat food when it is about six months old. This huge animal eats tiny shrimp-like animals called krill. This is the same food its mother eats. Whales eat tons of krill every day. Blue whales have large layers of baleen instead of teeth. Baleen is the same material as human fingernails. It is like a big comb. The whale takes a huge gulp of water. The baleen lets the water escape but keeps the krill inside to be eaten.

The baby blue whale will grow up to be the largest animal in the world. Blue whales are larger than even the largest dinosaurs that once walked the earth. They can measure up to 100 feet long. That is about as long as three school buses. Blue whales are not only the largest, but also the loudest, animals on earth. Scientists think blue whales can hear each other from a thousand miles away. Someday the baby blue whale will be grown. As it glides through the oceans, will it sing out to its mother from a far distance? For now, we can only wonder.

Name: ______________________________

Dictionary

Look at the picture. Read the word.
Write the word on the line.

Content Vocabulary

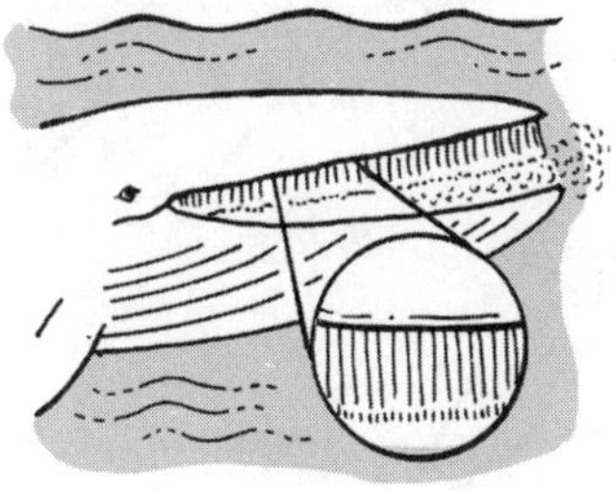

baleen

____

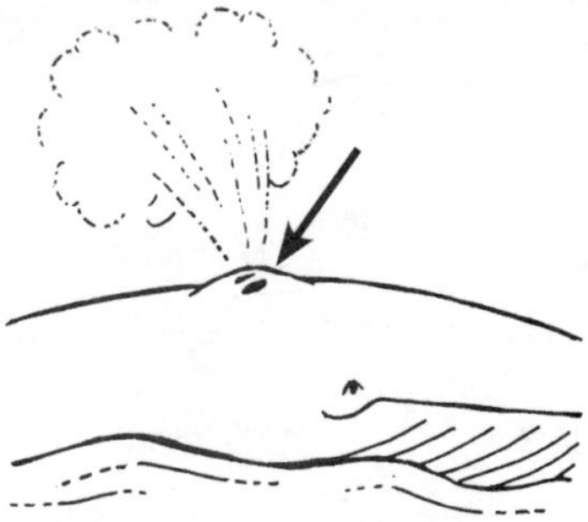

blowholes

____

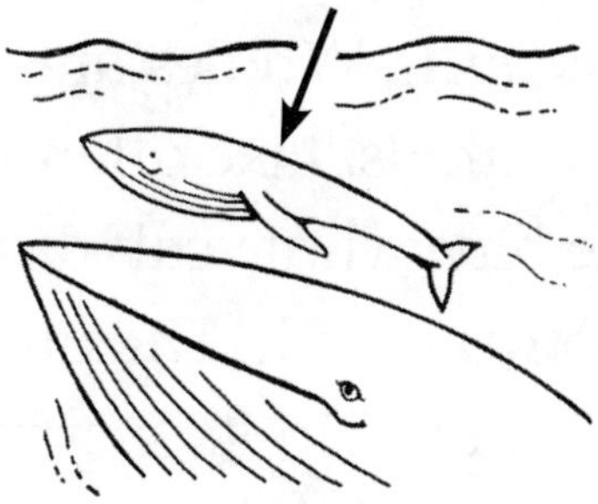

calf

____

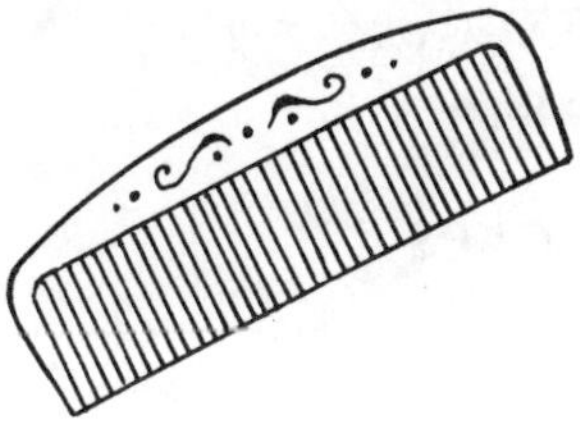

comb

____

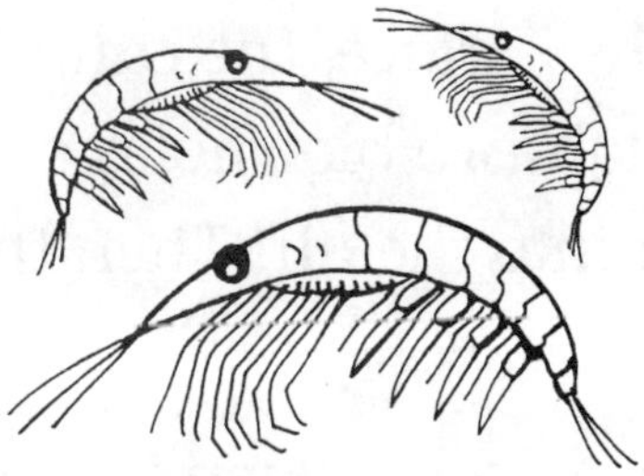

krill

____

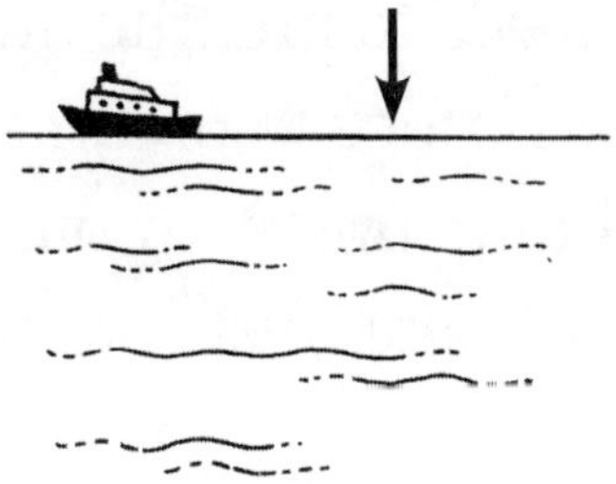

surface

____

Words to Know

adult	breath	breathe	fingernails
layers	mammal	mist	ocean
pounds	shrimp	weigh	

Name: ______________________________

Baby Blue Whale

The largest baby animal in the world is the baby blue whale. A blue whale calf can weigh up to three tons when it is born. Whales are mammals. Like all mammals, the blue whale calf drinks its mother's milk. The milk is very rich in fat. In its first year, the baby blue whale grows 200 pounds a day. Wow!

When it is born, the mother blue whale pushes her calf to the ocean's surface for its first breath. Just like its mother, it needs to breathe air. Then every few minutes, it swims to the surface to breathe. At the surface, the calf breathes out. It blows misty air out through two blowholes on top of its head. The mist sprays high into the air! Then the calf takes in more air through its blowholes.

The whale calf starts to eat food when it is about six months old. Just like its mother, it eats tiny shrimp-like animals called krill. Blue whales have layers of baleen instead of teeth. Baleen is made of the same stuff as fingernails. It is like a big comb. The whale takes a huge gulp of ocean water. The baleen lets the water out, but not the krill.

Adult blue whales can be up to 100 feet long. That is about as long as three school buses! Adult blue whales are the largest animals in the world.

Name: ______________________________

I Read and Understand

Read and answer.

1. A baby blue whale grows _____.
   - ❍ 200 pounds a day
   - ❍ 200 pounds a month
   - ❍ 200 pounds a year

2. A blue whale has two _____.
   - ❍ teeth
   - ❍ school buses
   - ❍ blowholes

3. All mammals _____.
   - ❍ can swim fast
   - ❍ are very large
   - ❍ drink their mother's milk

4. A blue whale calf eats and breathes _____.
   - ❍ underwater
   - ❍ like its mother
   - ❍ like a fish

5. The world's largest baby animal is a _____.
   - ❍ shrimp
   - ❍ blue whale
   - ❍ baleen

Name: ____________________

I Read Closely

Read the text closely.
Finish the sentence with the words used in the text.

1. When the calf breathes out, the mist

____

____

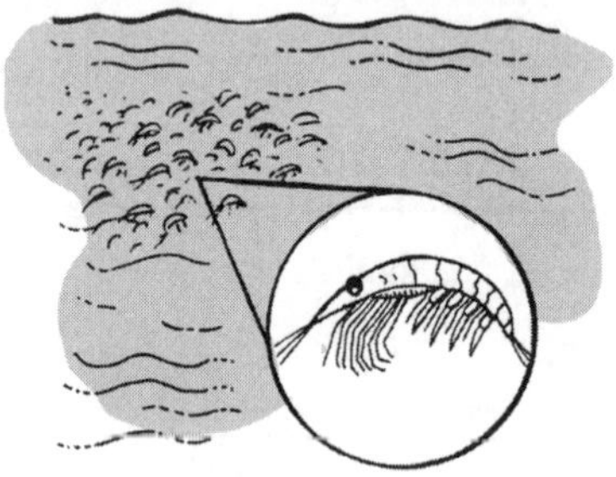

2. It eats tiny ____________________

____

____

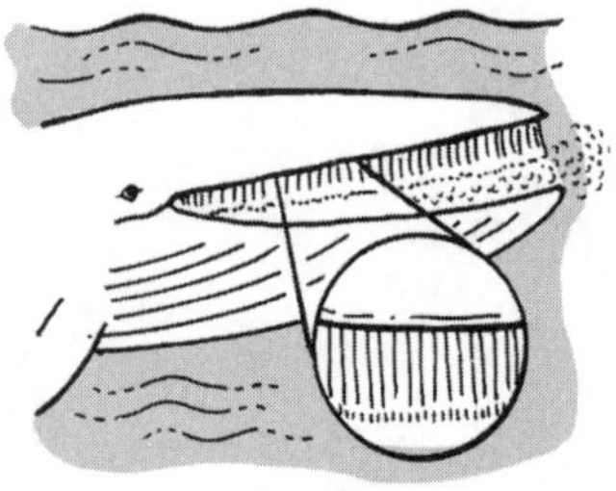

3. Blue whales have layers of

____

____

4. Adult blue whales are about as long as

____

____

Name: ______________________________

Words I Know

Read and answer.

1. A _____ sprays from a whale's blowholes.
   - ❍ mist
   - ❍ krill
   - ❍ baleen

2. Krill are like tiny _____.
   - ❍ minutes
   - ❍ shrimp
   - ❍ sprays

3. A blue whale has _____ instead of teeth.
   - ❍ baleen
   - ❍ pounds
   - ❍ largest

4. A blue whale swims to the _____ to get air.
   - ❍ comb
   - ❍ breath
   - ❍ surface

5. Blue whales have two _____.
   - ❍ pounds
   - ❍ blowholes
   - ❍ fingernails

6. The blue whale eats _____.
   - ❍ krill
   - ❍ baleen
   - ❍ mammals

Name: ______________________

I Can Write

Choose one topic. Write three facts about baby blue whales.

Topics

its size **how it eats** **how it breathes**

1. ______________________________

2. ______________________________

3. ______________________________

Draw a picture to show how a blue whale calf is like its parents.

Name: ______________________

What I Learned

Write a paragraph that tells about baby blue whales.
Use the facts from your *I Can Write* page.